ANIMALS OF TASMANIA

First published in Australia in 2009
by Quintus Publishing,
an imprint of the University of Tasmania,
School of English, Journalism and European Languages,
Private Bag 82, Hobart, Tasmania, Australia 7001.
www.quintus.utas.edu.au

Cataloguing-in-Publication details are available from the
National Library of Australia
www.librariesaustralia.nla.gov.au

ISBN 978-0-9775572-7-1

Designer: Tracey Allen
Editor: Janine Flew
Typeset in Caslon 10/13 pt
Colour reproduction by Photolith
Printed in Australia by Focal Printing Tasmania

ANIMALS OF TASMANIA
WILDLIFE OF AN INCREDIBLE ISLAND

Sally Bryant and Tim Squires

CONTENTS

TASMANIA

TRULY & ABSOLUTELY

AN INCREDIBLE ISLAND

* Really try to convey the notion of **deep** geological time

for example: Tasmania's links to the ancient supercontinent of Gondwana

CONTINENTAL DRIFT

RISING / FALLING SEA LEVELS = UNIQUE WILDLIFE

EVOLUTION / SPECIATION

Flinders Island

Cape Barren Island

Clarke Island

C. Naturaliste

Eddystone Point

Bay of Fires

St Helens

St Helens Point

Devonport

Mt Arthur

Launceston

St Marys

Bicheno

HIGHLANDS

MIDLANDS

Queenstown

Strahan

Frenchmans Cap

Macquarie Harbour

Swansea

Freycinet

Orford

Maria Island

Lake Pedder

Hobart

Arthur Range

Hartz Mt.

Tasman Peninsula

Bathurst Harbour

Bruny Island

S.W. Cape

South East Cape

TASMAN SEA

South-Eastern Australia

King Island

Flinders Island

Tasmania

Coastline before rise of sea level

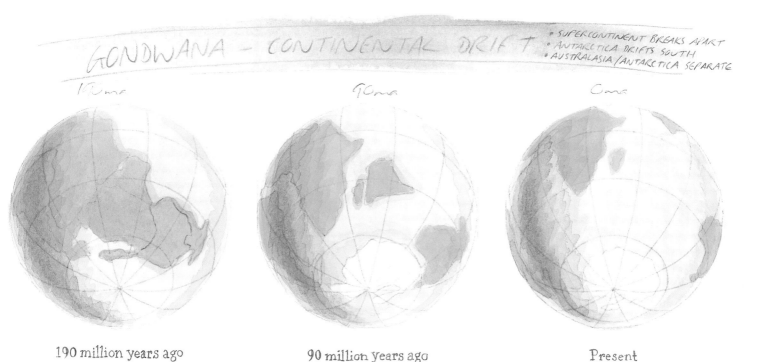

GONDWANA — CONTINENTAL DRIFT
• SUPERCONTINENT BREAKS APART
• ANTARCTICA DRIFTS SOUTH
• AUSTRALASIA/ANTARCTICA SEPARATE

190 million years ago   90 million years ago   Present

HOW IT ALL BEGAN

Our understanding of how Tasmania became an island inhabited by so many unique species has, like the species themselves, evolved over time. The story of island biogeography is both complex and simple, and even though volumes have been written on this fascinating subject, there is always more to learn.

About 300 million years ago, all our present continents were merged as one great land mass called Pangaea. Over time, due to dynamic forces deep within the earth's crust, Pangaea began to break into pieces. One piece, called Laurasia, floated north and eventually became the continents of Asia, Europe and North America. The other piece, Gondwana, drifted across the ocean for millions of years until eventually Africa and India broke free. Gradually, South America and New Zealand broke away and headed to the east. The final separation occurred about 38 million years ago, with Australia rotating north and Antarctica moving south towards the pole. The great landmasses of the world as we know it were born and settling into position.

This series of complex geological events allows us to trace the radiation of species as they migrated around the globe. By walking, flying or hitching a ride, plants and animals dispersed across the landscape, some finding favourable new destinations, others dying out along the way. Some faunal groups, such as the marsupials, were highly successful and spread from their place of origin in South America to at one time occupy nearly every major country in the world. When marsupials finally arrived in Australia, the environmental conditions were ideal and they gradually evolved into the modern descendants we know today (Dickman & Woodford Ganf 2007). Of course, in geological time, this happened only yesterday.

Crossing the bridge

Tasmania has always been part of Australia. Less than 200 km wide, Bass Strait has shaped Tasmania's biodiversity over millions of years, being alternately a land bridge or a barrier of water. At the height of the last great ice age, the sea was much lower than it is today and Bass Strait was transformed into a cold, windswept desert of calcarenite and siliceous sands stretching from northern Tasmania into southern Victoria. Islands in the Furneaux Group were high points in a route that could be walked between Cape Portland and Wilson's Promontory. Islands to the west around the Hunter Group provided cross-country passage between Cape Otway and the northwest tip of Tasmania. Cool, wet rainforest of Myrtle and Celery-top Pine grew over King Island, whereas temperate eucalypt forest covered the more mountainous peaks to the east (Harris *et al.* 2001). The Yarra River flowed from Victoria's valley floor into Lake Bass and overflowed into the mouth of the Tamar River. Tasmania and mainland Australia were intimately connected.

For thousands of years, animals and humans moved freely across this land bridge and many found Tasmania's cooler maritime climate ideal. Some were quick to establish permanent populations, while others continued to migrate back and forth. But as the climate warmed, the glaciers and ice caps melted, and about 12,000 years ago the Bassian land bridge had reverted to sea. The mountain ranges to the west and east of Bass Strait became stepping-stones and Tasmania itself once again became Australia's largest island.

This warming climate affected the entire Australian landscape and large arid zones and inland deserts were formed. Animals once dependent on lush, wet habitats avoided extinction by reducing their body size through natural selection, or moving further south. Giant species, such as Australia's megafauna, were too slow to adapt and either died out naturally or were more easily hunted by Aborigines for food. Our megafauna were super-sized creatures such as the giant echidna *Zaglossus harrissoni*, which was more than a metre in length, and the marsupial lion *Thylacoleo* sp. and giant kangaroo *Protemnodon anak*, both of which were much larger still (Hope 1974). Within a relatively short period, all were extinct, leaving behind only traces of their fascinating story in cave deposits and windblown sands.

Animals once widespread on mainland Australia, such as Tasmania's Thylacine and Native-hen, began to contract their ranges and to push further to the south. Populations of both these species and many others became extinct on the mainland soon after the dingo arrived, about 3500 years ago, whereas the Tasmanian Devil hung on in the southwest corner of Western Australia until about 430 years ago (Dickman & Woodford Ganf 2007). The Tasmanian Pademelon, Bettong and Eastern Quoll all survived in the southeast of Victoria until the early 1900s, before going extinct (DCE 1992).

Tasmania's island separation has produced an eclectic mix of fauna. Some animals have been living here since the island's ancient relic past, while others are more recently arrived. As a consequence of the flooding, some are now stranded here at the edge of their natural range. Whatever their place of origin, all these species have melded into the Tasmanian environment and continued to evolve their own dynamic and enduring ways of life.

Naturally special

Islands all over the world are special. Their life forms evolve into the smallest, largest or most unusual of their kind. Surrounded by water, islands are a window to evolution through their limiting size and enforced isolation. Madagascar, Galapagos, Hawaii and New Zealand are islands all famous for their rich faunal histories and struggles of survival. Islands are centres of endemism, faunal collapse and species extinction. Tasmania is one of those places.

Tasmania is a little over 64,000 square km in area, with a coastline 4700 km long. Dotted offshore are more than 300 smaller islands and rock stacks, defining the island's boundary with great contrast and natural beauty. This is a mountainous place with spectacular vistas and highly varied vegetation. At the higher altitudes are alpine heaths and fjaeldmark surrounded by pockets of sphagnum peatlands. The lower valleys are dominated by dense rainforest of Myrtle *Nothofagus cunninghamii*, Celery Top Pine *Phyllocladus aspleniifolius*, Sassafras *Atherosperma moschatum* and Leatherwood *Eucryphia lucida*. Along secluded riverbanks are stands of Huon Pine *Lagarostrobos franklinii*, some specimens of which are so ancient the entire climatic history of the southern hemisphere is captured within their fibre. Dominating the eastern region are sclerophyll forests, grassy woodland and heaths containing flora that is more typically Australian, such as Wattle and Banksia. Exquisite treasures are strewn across the land, such as tiny orchids, mosses and liverworts and the self-cloning King's Lomatia *Lomatia tasmanica*, the oldest living plant on earth. Tasmania's great wild rivers with their tannin-stained waters flow amid ancient soils that are the glue holding it all together.

Macquarie Island also forms part of Tasmania's territorial lands and although it lies about 1500 km southeast of Hobart, this amazing sub-Antarctic platform is recognised by World Heritage status for its geological formation. Macquarie Island is home to a staggering biomass of plant and animal life and is a place like no other.

Spectacular wildlife

What makes Tasmania even more remarkable is its wildlife. Tasmania has eighty-six species of mammal, of which forty-two are native and live in non-marine environments. Six species and fifteen subspecies are endemic. One of these, the Thylacine, is now extinct, although tragically, more appear to be following. More than 200 species of bird are either resident or regularly visit these shores (SDAC 1996). Four species are now extinct (King Island Emu, Tasmanian Emu, Macquarie Island Rail and Macquarie Island Parakeet), and yet again, tragically, more appear to be following. The northeast region is a hotspot for reptile diversity, with eighteen of Tasmania's twenty-one native species, such as the

She-oak Skink *Cyclodomorphus casuarinae* (named after a boat, not a tree) and the Ocellated Skink *Niveoscincus ocellatus*, still found there in relative abundance (Hutchinson *et al.* 2001). The endemic Mountain Skink *N. orocryptus* and Northern and Southern Snow Skinks *N. greeni* and *N. microlepidotus* penetrate the subalpine areas, a challenging environment for creatures reliant on warmth. Many of Tasmania's tree frogs, marsh frogs, toadlets and the more recently discovered Moss Froglet *Bryobatrachus nimbus* flourish in wetlands, or just damp, muddy places along the sides of roads. Twenty-five species of native fish live in Tasmania's freshwater systems and many are dependent on just one body of water for their survival. Of these, twelve are endemic, with ten belonging to the family Galaxiidae alone, reflecting a staggeringly high level of endemism that is typical of small islands. Tasmania's diverse wildlife attracts visitors from around the world, who see this place as a natural wonderland and stronghold for wildlife conservation and survival.

GROUP	NATIVE SPECIES	ENDEMIC	THREATENED **	EXTINCT
Mammal	42	6	6	1
Bird	212*	14 – 16 †	36	4
Reptile	21	7	3	0
Amphibian	11	3	2	0
Freshwater Fish	25	12	12	nearly 1

* Bird numbers are plus or minus some migratory waders and infrequent visitors.
** Listed in State and Commonwealth threatened species legislation in 2009.
† Endemic birds include species that breed in Tasmania.

(or land bridge islands)

THINK ABOUT: CONTINENTAL VS OCEANIC ISLANDS / INSULAR EVOLUTION PROS & CONS

"The species of all kinds which inhabit oceanic islands are few in number compared with those on equal continental areas" – CHARLES DARWIN *The Origin of Species* (Species/area relationship?)

CONTINENTAL ISLANDS

Examples:

Tasmania, Madagascar, Bali, Sri Lanka, New Guinea

Characteristics:

* Lie relatively close to neighbouring mainlands
* Share same continental shelf with mainlands
* Surrounded by relatively shallow water
* Throughout their history have been periodically subjected to reconnection with their mainlands via land bridges during periods of lowered sea level

OCEANIC ISLANDS

Examples:

Hawaii, Mauritius, Reunion, Galapagos Archipelago,

Characteristics

* Much more remote – far away from mainlands
* Do not sit on continental shelves
* Often formed by volcanic activity – rise up from deep ocean floors – surrounded by deep water
* Have never had any connection to another major land mass / continent.
* Often very much younger than continental islands.

The most fundamental biological distinction is that oceanic islands begin their existence completely devoid of terrestrial forms of life, whereas continental islands are usually heavily populated with the species they once shared with their parent mainlands before they became isolated.

warm grey   red brown   light orange   chartreuse   lemon yellow   light yellow   pastel yellow   saffron yellow   deep ochre   yellow ochre

It's always about people

Aborigines crossed into Tasmania about 60,000 years ago via the Bassian land bridge, and soon adapted to their newfound environment. Archaeological evidence in Kutikina (meaning 'spirit') Cave and Deene Reena Cave in southwest Tasmania shows how Aboriginal people used sophisticated stone tools to prepare wallabies and wombats and cook them over charcoal fires. Tasmania's indigenous people (Palawa) developed a deep understanding of and intimate connection with the wildlife, as a resource and an integral part of their culture. Ceremonies and seasonal movement of tribes revolved around key species and local dialects described those animals most important to them. All kinds of mammals were eaten, as were birds and eggs, and the Short-tailed Shearwater *Puffinus tenuirostris*, called 'yolla', was harvested annually. Seals were corralled onshore, and the women dived expertly for shellfish, which they carried in their coiled fibre baskets (tayenebe). For decoration or symbolic purposes, many people wore strands of tiny green mariner shells or animal sinew around their neck, and in the winter they would drape a cloak of kangaroo skin around their shoulders. Over thousands of years a dynamic relationship existed, but at some point that had to change.

The British arrived in Australia with fervour and purpose. Their priority was to stake their claim and settle the land, and even though the Antipodes were a veritable treasure trove, their focus was more on outmanoeuvring the French than on natural history collection. It was the French who made detailed scientific discoveries of Tasmania, especially the expeditions of Bruny d'Entrecasteaux and Nicolas Baudin. From their anchorages along the east coast, small boats sallied forth collecting, comparing and sketching the indigenous plants, animals and people in this strange new land. Naturalists like Péron, Labillardière and Lesueur were the first to collect many of Tasmania's native species, which were dutifully lodged in the museums of France and provided invaluable scientific reference material for centuries to come.

When Van Diemen's Land was settled in 1803, it seemed the perfect place to send convicts and sheep and to value the wildlife in terms of food and fur. It took quite some time before interest in the island's natural history grew, or at least reached any respectable level. But grow it did, and through the efforts of many well-known naturalists, especially Ronald Gunn, Thomas Ewing and Col. William Legge, and visiting scientists such as Charles Darwin and John Gould, the profile of Tasmania's fauna grew and its uniqueness in the scientific world began to attract attention and recognition. Although Charles Darwin recollected Hobart Town as an inferior place after his brief stopover in 1836 on board the HMS *Beagle*, he nonetheless made detailed natural history observations and marvelled at the great 'Eucalypti' and noble forest shrouded in mist on the slopes of Mt Wellington. The masterful birdman John Gould arrived in 1838 and stayed for several months, amassing hundreds of animal specimens and eventually describing more than thirty of them (Hindwood 1938).

Given Gould's involvement in Darwin's theory of evolution, it's tantalising to wonder whether Tasmania could have earned a reputation for variation in thornbills, as the Galapagos did for finches.

It was not until 1843 that the first systematic list of Tasmanian mammals, compiled by J. E. Gray, made any serious attempt at unravelling the haphazard scientific collections that had been sent to the British Museum. But from here on, institutions such as the Royal Society of Van Diemen's Land (later Tasmania), the University of Tasmania, the Tasmanian Museum and the Queen Victoria Museum eventually laid the foundations for documenting Tasmania's faunal inventory in an international and academically acceptable way.

Meanwhile, in the recesses of the Tasmanian bush, the keen-eyed and resourceful early settlers were also studying the wildlife and learning which native animals were useful and which were not. Their knowledge of how to trap, skin, cook or tame the wildlife improved their quality of life and their ability to survive in what must have seemed a hostile environment. They collected tadpoles and eggs, mended broken wings, raised joeys, and seemingly all hated snakes. 'Lady Jane Franklin, during the government of her husband, Sir John Franklin, with her wonted liberality and kindness of heart offered a reward of one shilling per head for every snake killed throughout the island. During the first year she paid about £700 for nearly 14,000 snakes killed. Subsequently she discontinued this reward, having ascertained that it would not at that time prove beneficial in ridding the island of the pest' (West 1852). The new colony was bound to prosper.

And so the story continues. This island's attachment to its wildlife has been fostered over many generations and is embedded in folklore and culture. But, as in so many other places, Tasmania's wildlife and natural systems are under enormous pressure and threat. Development, feral pests, disease and our demand for the luxuries of life are akin to the nineteenth century's need for oil as fuel and feathers to adorn ladies' hats. The situation in which we find ourselves today is still a part of the human desire for progress.

Tasmania's people are like its wildlife. Whether indigenous or more newly arrived, all are somehow connected to this land, with rich layers of history and stories to tell. Perhaps only now are we realising that we alone control the fate of one of the most naturally important places on the planet.

THYLACINE

(Tasmanian Tiger)
Thylacinus cynocephalus

'154. A reward of One Pound shall be payable out of the Consolidated Revenue for the destruction of every full-grown Native Tiger (Thylacinus cynocephalus), and the sum of Ten Shillings for every half-grown or young Native Tiger, subject to the following conditions ...'
(excerpt from Government Bounty Records 1888)

The story of the Thylacine – an animal which the naturalist John Gould prophesised was doomed to extinction – is full of tragedy and irony.

The early years of settlement were a time to clear and farm the land, not to ponder the fate of the native wildlife. In 1888, the Tasmanian Parliament joined with the Van Diemen's Land Company in offering a bounty to rid the colony of the 'wolf dog', a cursed animal that killed livestock and was damaging the sheep industry. From 1888 to 1909 more than 2000 bounties were paid for adult and cub Thylacines, although this is a gross underestimate of the number of animals actually destroyed. History now records how the world's largest marsupial carnivore, the Thylacine, was trapped, poisoned and shot to extinction:

'... on the east coast 17 adult tigers and a number of pups were killed in one day ... shot four tigers in the scrub ... on reaching Kings Bay the tigers took to the water and were shot. The young ones would not follow and were clubbed and killed by dogs ... his father caught about 20 ... as many as 70, because they were sheep killers ... one of the boys got one home alive. He sent it to Launceston where a man offered him £5 for it but he reduced the price because it was a small one ...' (extracts from Sharland 1971)

Thylacinus cynocephalus derives from the Latin 'pouched dog with wolf head'. Fossil evidence shows that Thylacines were once in New Guinea and across the entire Australian continent. They would have entered Tasmania between 40,000 and 12,000 years ago by crossing the Bassian land bridge that joined with what is now southern Victoria. Aboriginal rock paintings depict a stripy tiger alongside kangaroos and emus, and mummified carcases dating back to 3280 BC have been discovered in Western Australian caves (Owen 2003). When the dingo arrived into northern Australia, a significant new competitor entered the scene. Thylacines began to contract their range by heading further and further to the south but they could no longer seek refuge in what is now Tasmania, as Bass Strait had flooded by then. Eventually they died out on the mainland, whereas those surviving in Tasmania were safe and able to fulfil their ecological role as a top-order predator.

Thylacines were widespread but never numerous in Tasmania. They preferred lightly timbered woodland and grassy plains where wallabies were abundant. 'Most of the daylight hours are spent by this species in some chosen cave amidst the rocks of the higher hills or mountains, and with the approach of night it sallies forth to the valleys and plains in search of prey. It cannot, however, be considered a strictly nocturnal animal, for they are occasionally seen abroad in the daylight' (Lord & Scott 1924). They were not a particularly fast or agile creature, but relied on ambush or exhausting their prey by relentless pursuit.

With their enormous jaws they could seize a wallaby by the shoulder or chest and with their long canine teeth, puncture and kill it. Farmers said that Thylacines ate the soft tissues first and only consumed a little of what they killed, never returning to a carcase.

Fully grown Thylacines measured about 2 m from the nose to the tip of the tail, were 50 cm high at the shoulder and could be up to 25 kg in weight. Lord and Scott (1924) describe their general character as 'Large and wolf-like. Muzzle long and slender. Fur short. General colour tawny greyish brown, below paler. The posterior part of the back is marked with 16–18 dark chocolate coloured bands. The tail gradually merges into the body and is shorter than same. The young have more pronounced stripes and a distinct crest on the tail'. Thylacines had five front toes arranged symmetrically around the footpad, although the fifth was raised and rarely left an impression. Their gait was a stiff trot or canter while holding their semi-rigid tail erect. They made a yap or high-pitched bark, quite different to that of any other animal, and apparently the noise sent hunting dogs wild with excitement.

The female gave birth to embryonic young that developed in her rear-opening pouch. Up to four cubs could be raised in a year and once they grew too large for the pouch they were left in a well-hidden den, deep in the rocks or thick vegetation. At weaning time, the juveniles would emerge from the den, their long tails not yet rigid, and scramble behind the mother as she taught them how to hunt. It is likely that Thylacines lived for eight to ten years in the wild.

Dr Eric Guiler provides accounts of trappers who caught 'dozens of them useless things', and during the late 1880s to early 1900s the species was still relatively easy to obtain (Guiler 1985). Mary Roberts displayed them at her private zoo Beaumaris at Battery Point, and while she created a marketable trade in Thylacines she also fought for their protection, even promoting the role zoos could play in captive breeding programs (Guiler 1986). Although they were keenly sought by zoos around the world it was said that they never made good exhibits, as they were poorly suited to life in a pen and did little to please the visitor. London Zoo made the last Thylacine purchase in 1926, paying the hefty sum of £150, a huge amount compared to the meagre government bounty. The animal died a few years later. By 1936, Thylacines had become so rare that the species was added to Tasmania's list of protected wildlife. Ironically, this was the year in which 'Benjamin', the last known living Thylacine, died at the Beaumaris Zoo, which had since relocated from Battery Point to the Hobart Domain. Benjamin had been on display for twelve years and seven months and in its latter years was described as being an old, mangy-looking animal. The Tasmanian Government identified De Witt Island and Maria Island as potential Thylacine sanctuaries and began stocking them with food species, but it was far too late, as no more Thylacines were ever found.

Even though alleged sightings continue, the chances of finding Thylacines have long gone, any remnant pockets probably dying out by the 1960s or 70s. What lives on is the story of a deliberate and brutal extinction and a curious disbelief that this tragedy occurred not so very long ago. A pair of Thylacines flank Tasmania's Coat of Arms, which depicts the fruits of harvest and the motto 'Fertility and Faithfulness'.

TASMANIAN DEVIL

Sarcophilus harrisii

In 1916 'Corporal Bluey' became the mascot of the 12th/40th Battalion; his serial number was TX666. During ceremonial occasions he wore a specially made coat and was held by an officer wearing long white gloves. His battalion was the first regiment to leave Tasmania as part of the Australian Imperial Force during World War One. They were sent to the Western Front and at Flanders fought with bravery and honour in the bloody battle of Broodseinde Ridge. How much action Corporal Bluey saw is debatable, but what he didn't see, he probably created.

In the dead of night, the sounds of blood-curdling screams, ripping flesh and gnashing teeth must have sent fear into the hearts of Tasmania's early settlers, for surely this place was possessed by demons, devils and banshees. Cunning and ferocious, they roamed in secret, thieving poultry, killing lambs, eating old boots and jackets, including the buttons. In 1808, George Prideaux Harris, after whom the species is named, published this brief account: 'These animals were very common on our first settling at Hobart Town, and were particularly destructive to poultry, &c. They, however, furnished the convicts with a fresh meal, and the flesh was said to be not unlike veal. As the settlement increased, and the ground became cleared, they were driven from their haunts near the town to the deeper recesses of the forest yet unexplored' (Troughton 1967). Harris originally ascribed the Tasmanian Devil the family name *Didelphis*, but this was later changed to the Greek *Sarcophilus*, meaning 'flesh-loving'. Harris – editor of the colony's first newspaper, the *Van Diemen's Land Intelligencer* – could, if he wished, have added that when hot or stressed the devil's ears flush bright red, like the horns of Satan; but the newspaper folded when the colony ran out of paper.

In 1895, Tasmania's first zoo opened in the grounds of a stately home called Beaumaris at Battery Point. The owner, Mrs Mary Roberts, was particularly fond of her Tasmanian Devils and was the first to breed them in captivity. She published an account of her observations and in 1915 finished her manuscript by saying, 'I have derived much pleasure from studying the habits and disposition of the Tasmanian devil, and have found that they respond to kindness and certainly show affection and pleasure when I approach them. Others who do not know or understand them may think as they like, but I who love them, and have considerable experience in keeping most of our marsupials from Thylacine to the opossum mouse, will always regard them as first favourites – my little black play mates.'

Unfortunately not everyone regarded the Tasmanian Devil with the same affection as Mary Roberts. In fact, many thought them so loathsome and disgusting that they deserved to be shot; after all, we had rid the colony of the Thylacine, so the devil had better not overstep the mark. For almost the next hundred years the Tasmanian Devil was either persecuted, ridiculed or largely ignored, with little regard paid to its scientific uniqueness or its functional role in the ecosystem.

Although the Tasmanian Devil is a carnivore and can easily kill prey many times its own size, its talent is more for finding food than killing food. Devils can travel up to 10 km a night in search of carrion and with their acute sense of smell can locate a dead body up to 2 km away. With their powerful jaws and vice-like grip, they can devour any kind of carcase, eating everything, including fur, bone and guts.

Feeding can be a social event. The sound of one devil ripping flesh can attract others to the scene, which in turn triggers frenzied bouts of spitting, hissing and swearing, for if there's one thing devils don't do well, it's share.

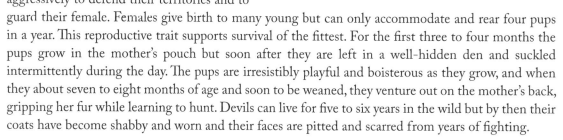

They are strongly built animals, and adult males can weigh up to 13 kg and females up to 9 kg. They are black in colour, many sporting an individual white blaze across the chest, and with a scrawny tail with a wispy end. While at times highly social, devils are more often solitary and territorial in nature, and during the breeding season males will fight aggressively to defend their territories and to guard their female. Females give birth to many young but can only accommodate and rear four pups in a year. This reproductive trait supports survival of the fittest. For the first three to four months the pups grow in the mother's pouch but soon after they are left in a well-hidden den and suckled intermittently during the day. The pups are irresistibly playful and boisterous as they grow, and when they about seven to eight months of age and soon to be weaned, they venture out on the mother's back, gripping her fur while learning to hunt. Devils can live for five to six years in the wild but by then their coats have become shabby and worn and their faces are pitted and scarred from years of fighting.

Up until the 1990s Tasmanian Devils were common and widespread, with a population estimated at about 150,000 (Nick Mooney pers. comm.). But then everything changed. In 1996, devils were found with horrendous facial tumours, caused by a new type of infectious cancer. The cancer starts as a small lesion around the mouth and quickly grows to erode the jaw, leading to an inevitable and agonising death. Devil Facial Tumour Disease (DFTD) is transmitted through biting and somehow it alters the animal's chromosome structure, making its own defence system incapable of fighting the disease. What triggered the cancer is still unknown but the disease is now widespread and the devil population has plummeted.

The Tasmanian Devil has become a nationally endangered species and the world is learning of its plight. The Save the Devil program is well under way and involves a range of recovery actions, including captive breeding, disease suppression trials and field monitoring. The public's desire to save the species is overwhelming, as for many it has become the symbol of this place. It is the underdog, the persecuted, the crazy character, and it's tough; and to the people who live here, it's a survivor, just like us.

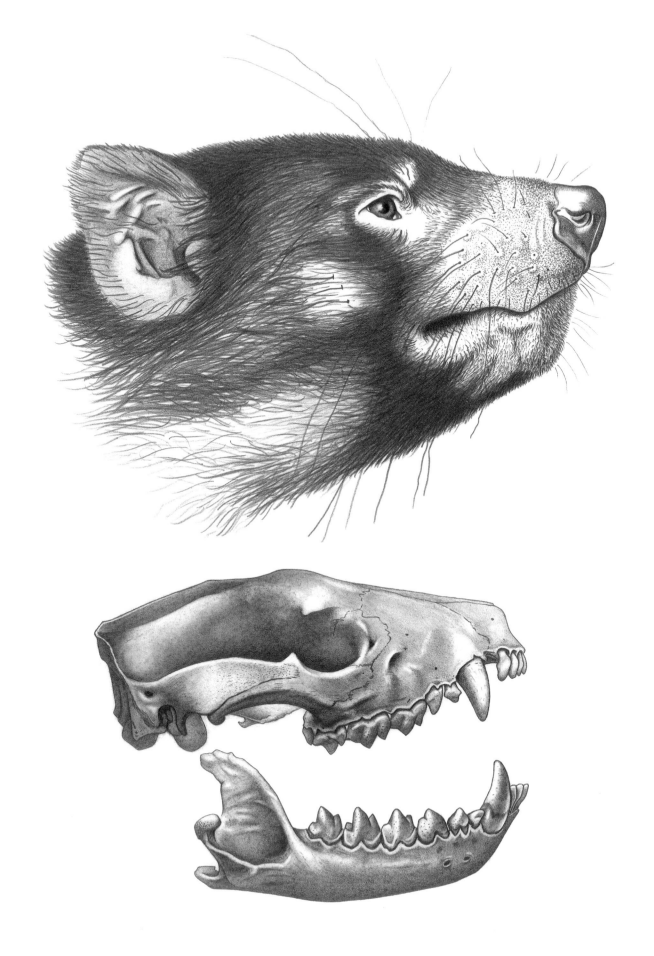

SPOTTED-TAILED QUOLL

Dasyurus maculatus maculatus

There is something haunting about the Spotted-tailed Quoll; not the animal itself, but its long-term future. This species has a long history of decline, and now, as Tasmania's other large predators spiral to extinction, there is uncertainty about its survival.

Spotted-tailed Quolls once occurred throughout eastern and southeastern Australia but are now extremely rare. Their range in Victoria has more than halved over recent years and they are no longer found in South Australia. Fossil evidence shows that they were once widespread on the islands of Bass Strait but were extinct there by 1923. The last Bass Strait record was of them being on King Island but they were eventually destroyed by the early settlers for killing their poultry and damaging animals caught on snare lines (Donaghey 2003). Throughout the twentieth century, Spotted-tailed Quolls were most often seen along Tasmania's north coast and in forested areas in the Gordon, King and Huon river catchments (Bryant & Jackson 1999), but nowhere were they common and since then they have continued to decline in range.

Captain Arthur Phillip, first governor of New South Wales, called this animal the spotted marten and, while all the Dasyurus have spots on their body, only this species has spots on the tail. Phillip remarked that they were not only very ferocious but also exceedingly stubborn (Troughton 1967). While this may be true, Spotted-tailed Quolls are also naturally curious and any that live near bushwalking huts will spontaneously appear as soon as the lunch packs are opened. They are solitary creatures with large home ranges and some individuals have been radio-tracked travelling more than 20 km in a night (Jones *et al.* 2001). They can be active at night or during the day and are expert climbers. With their serrated footpad and first toe, they are agile in the treetops, stalking birds or rifling nests for chicks and eggs. They will eat just about anything from carrion and insects to small or medium-sized mammals up to 4 kg in weight – or half their own body weight.

So why should an animal as versatile as this be in decline? One answer lies in their inherent rarity. Spotted-tailed Quolls live to no more than about four years of age, which is a short life span for an animal the size of a large cat. They are sexually mature by one year of age but generally do not breed until they are two. They have a strictly seasonal breeding cycle and although the female can suckle up to six young, the average litter size is less, and this declines even further as she becomes older (Jones *et al.* 2001).

Compared to other Dasyurus, Spotted-tailed Quolls are a distinctly ancestral and separate form (Jones *et al.* 2001). They are incapable of adapting quickly to change either physiologically, due to their low reproductive rate and short life span, or behaviourally, as they are solitary with a naturally large home range. Once the Thylacine, Tasmanian Devil and Wedge-tailed Eagle dominated the Tasmanian landscape as top-order predators, but these species are now either extinct or drastically in decline. As this predatory niche becomes available, sadly the last potential native candidate is unlikely to be able to fill it. Those who have seen old cinema footage of the Thylacine may have noticed a distinct similarity to the Spotted-tailed Quoll. Maybe it's just a curious coincidence or due to the angle of the jaw line.

EASTERN QUOLL

Dasyurus viverrinus

The name 'Quoll' first appeared in Hawkesworth's 1773 edition of Captain James Cook's *Voyages on the H.M.S. Endeavour,* describing an animal collected somewhere on the east coast of Australia. Aborigines of the Murray River region in South Australia called them 'ng'rui moch', meaning 'many spots', but early settlers likened them to the civet or polecat, and superficially Eastern Quolls do appear catlike. But that's where the similarity ends.

Fossil evidence shows that Eastern Quolls once ranged from southern Queensland to the South Australian border and until the 1940s were apparently still common near Adelaide and Melbourne. Pressure from the dingo then later the fox helped bring about their demise and the last mainland specimen was reportedly killed in the 1960s at Vaucluse in Sydney, ironically hit by a car.

Now confined to Tasmania, Eastern Quolls are one of the few native species that have adapted well to agriculture and thrive in the bush–pasture ecotone. At night they scamper over paddocks searching for insects, rodents and other small creatures; by day, they sleep in a well-hidden den. Sometimes they deliberately scamper into chicken coops and make a delightful mess of the occupants, and in the past 'warfare has waged against them … for the toll they take of the settlers poultry' (Lord & Scott 1924). They are formidable hunters and can seize live prey by the back of the neck or throttle it using their sharp incisors. At other times they scavenge on carrion or feed almost entirely on corbie grubs and other pasture pests.

Eastern Quolls are solitary in nature and can range over 40 ha in a night, but wherever food is plentiful, dense populations can occur. In these situations, individuals retain their personal space through mutual avoidance and respect, advertising their presence by dabbing trails of urine or squatting upright and sniffing the air. When these behaviours fail then plenty of squabbling and chasing breaks out, but this seldom leads to prolonged conflict or serious injury.

Mating starts in late May, depending on the local weather conditions, and males compete aggressively for females, fighting with interlocked mouths, and hissing and screeching. Successful males will mate with a female, or sometimes two or three a season, while unsuccessful males hang around the outskirts waiting for another opportunity if litters are lost. Up to six young are born in June, each measuring about 5 mm in length and barely visible to the naked eye. By two months of age they are bulging in the pouch and have velvety fur and eyes about to open. The female now leaves them in a den while she forages at night, returning frequently to feed and nurture them (Bryant 1988). At about five months of age, the mischievous, bright-eyed youngsters emerge clinging to the mother's back while she teaches them how to hunt and, perhaps, to scamper close to chicken pens.

Eastern Quolls have magnificent spotted coats and are ideally camouflaged in the Tasmanian bush. They are either fawn grey or jet black in colour, both forms having white spots over the body but not on the tail, and both colour types can occur in the same litter. Adult males can weigh up to 1.5 kg but the more finely built female rarely reaches more than 1 kg in weight. During winter they lose body condition and by about four years of age, disease and parasites have taken their toll.

Bettongs dig for seeds, roots, bulbs and fungi.

Females sometimes give birth to 2 or 3 young each year.

Joey

20% Y
70% R
10% B

TASMANIAN BETTONG

Bettongia gaimardi

The Tasmanian Bettong is a fascinating yet little-known creature. The term 'bettong' is an Aboriginal word meaning small wallaby, whereas the species name *gaimardi* honours the French naturalist Joseph Paul Gaimard, who collected the first specimen in 1819 from Port Jackson in Victoria. At one time the Tasmanian Bettong occurred across southeast Australia, but less than a hundred years after it was first collected, it had become extinct on the mainland due to the impact of foxes, feral cats and a changing landscape (DCE 1992).

In Tasmania, bettongs occur throughout the eastern half of the state, favouring dry sclerophyll forests and woodlands, especially those with little or no understorey. Unlike all other species of wallaby, bettongs build a grass-lined nest which they sleep in during the day. These nests are used constantly over a period of weeks or months and are well hidden under logs or in thick sags and bushes. Nests are elaborately woven from material carried in the bettong's prehensile tail; one nest taken to the Tasmanian Museum was described as being 'made entirely of fibre-like strips of stringy bark, every scrap of which had been carried over a quarter of a mile in the grip of the curled up tail' (Troughton 1967).

Just on dark, bettongs emerge to search the forest floor for roots, tubers and their favourite food, fungi. Mycorrhizal fungi grow beneath the soil, forming due to a parasitic relationship with the roots of plants, mainly eucalypts. The fungi depend on the host plant to grow, and in turn the plant benefits from aeration of the soil and increased nutrients. When mature, the fungi's truffle-like fruit emits a strong odour, which is simply irresistible to bettongs. As the fruit passes through the bettong's gut, the spores remain undigested and are discarded in the faeces, and so the bettong becomes a vehicle for spore dispersal (Visoiu & Lloyd 2003). The inter-dependency between bettong, fungi and eucalypt health drives the ecology of Tasmania's sclerophyll forests and influences factors such as their capacity to regenerate after fire.

Tasmanian Bettongs are fiercely independent creatures and are typically 'quarrelsome and pugnacious; perhaps even bad tempered. It fights viciously with its kind …, males fight with males and with females … but as a rule she returns as much as she gets' (Sharland 1963). Only during the breeding season do they tolerate each other, but even then bettong lovemaking lacks any romance and is more of a wrestling match with kicking and biting. The female's reproductive cycle is finely tuned, with each phase conducted with military-like precision. The female gives birth to a single young and by the time the joey is about one hundred days old and fully furred, it's ready to leave the pouch. A change in its sucking behaviour has already triggered the development of a fertilised egg that has lain dormant in the mother's body, and this foetus is now ready to be born. As the joey vacates the pouch, the female gives birth and is ready to mate soon after (Rose 1987). This finely tuned breeding cycle enables the Tasmanian Bettong to rear up to three offspring per year, and as a species to maintain its status quo in a productive yet highly fire-prone forest environment.

Bettongs are a precious and little-known part of Tasmania's marsupial fauna. They are restricted in distribution and highly sensitive to disturbance and, if the fox becomes established here, will inevitably slide toward extinction.

TASMANIAN PADEMELON

(Red-bellied Pademelon)

Thylogale billardierii

In 1822 Professor A. G. Desmarest published a scientific account of the Tasmanian Pademelon from specimens held in the Museum of Natural History, Paris. The description honoured the name of the French naturalist Jacques de Labillardière, who collected the animals in 1792 while on the D'Entrecasteaux Expedition in search of La Pérouse. Desmarest assigned the genus name as *Kangurus*, but this was later changed to *Thylogale* to correspond to that of other small scrub wallabies, commonly called 'paddymalla' (Troughton 1967).

Tasmanian Pademelons were once common throughout southeastern South Australia, Victoria and Tasmania, but due to a combination of hunting pressure and impact from the dingo and fox, the species became extinct on mainland Australia soon after Europeans arrived. However, the species continued to flourish in Tasmania and during early settlement and the depression years, shooting and snaring Tasmanian Pademelons was the mainstay of many small rural communities. Their thick, luxurious skins were exported or used as rugs and quilts to adorn the house and their meat fed the family, even the dogs. The naturalist John Gould likened the pademelon to the rabbit, saying it was one of the best flavoured of small kangaroos, and that as its flesh was sweet and succulent, it would make an ideal animal to feed the growing population of Europe (Troughton 1967). Thankfully Europeans didn't develop a taste for pademelon flesh, as the species had a hard enough time sustaining the appetite of this growing colony.

In profile, Tasmanian Pademelons have a small head and comparatively large, dumpy body, giving them a hunched appearance. Males are broad and strong in the chest and can be up to twice as heavy (7 to 8 kg) as females (4 kg). Pademelon are shy creatures and while nocturnal in habit they sometimes graze during the day, but stay close to cover, ready to dart down well-beaten runways if disturbed. During spring and summer they feed on succulent short grasses, but as the seasons change they browse on fruits, ferns and low woody foliage. They are adept at manipulating food with their front paws, and as they chew, they frequently raise their head to reveal a sweet, gentle face.

Pademelon give birth around April to June to a tiny newborn, the size of a jellybean. Early descriptions perpetuated the belief that marsupial babies grew from the nipple in the pouch 'like apples on twigs', as it seemed inconceivable that something so underdeveloped could possibly have arisen from anywhere else. But it does; with rudimentary paddle-like limbs, the newborn crawls from the birth canal up the mother's stomach and into the pouch, where it develops safe and secure for the next seven months. When the joey is fully furred it is ready to vacate the pouch, but even after it does so it continues to be suckled by the mother and stays close by her side. She reassures her 'young at foot' with nudges and low clucking calls until it is weaned, by which time the maternal bonds are broken and both are independent.

Hundreds of thousands of pademelons are killed every year on Tasmania's roads or shot and poisoned in a futile attempt to reduce the impact of their browsing. But neither our onslaught nor the species' resilience has changed over the years and pademelons remain widespread and abundant. Thankfully on many properties they are still welcome; especially those on the rural fringe where the grass is green and the gates are open.

Long-tailed Mouse

View of underside of
right front paw

underside of
right rear paw

100% R   100% Y
100% B

50% R
25% B
25% Y

Fur: dark brown/grey above, paler below.

Tail very long

Section of tail
* note: dark above,
light below

LONG-TAILED MOUSE

Pseudomys higginsi

The Long-tailed Mouse is one of about twenty-seven species of native rodent found throughout Australia. *Pseudomys* is Greek, meaning 'false mouse', and is the name used to distinguish native mice from the introduced House Mouse *Mus*, which occurs worldwide. *Pseudomys* are a hugely successful group of rodents that originated somewhere in eastern Indonesia. They colonised Australia relatively recently, about 15 million years ago, and now occupy nearly every habitat from alpine slope to desert sands. The Long-tailed Mouse was once found in eastern New South Wales, Victoria and Tasmania, after moving across the Bassian land bridge, but disappeared from mainland Australia about 10,000 years ago, possibly as a result of a prolonged dry spell due to climate change (Driessen & Rose 1999).

The first live specimen of a Long-tailed Mouse was discovered at place called Kentishbury, now Sheffield, in 1883. It was collected by E. T. Higgins, a physician and natural history dealer, who had joined with the Hobart-born W. F. Petterd, a scientist and boot importer, on a mission to discover new animal species in Tasmania. Their efforts were well rewarded, for they identified not only this mouse, which they formally described (Higgins & Petterd 1883), but a host of other mammals, invertebrates and marine species, many of which now bear their names.

The most comprehensive work undertaken to date on the Long-tailed Mouse is that of Dr Bob Green during the 1960s, while he was curator at the Queen Victoria Museum in Launceston. Green trapped them, bred them and studied their habits, describing the species as 'lightly built, with a rather delicate and long-legged appearance which is accentuated by its nervous disposition and habit of making sudden evasive leaps' (Green 1968). If you combine these sudden evasive leaps with the species' ability to make 'a faint high-pitched whistle when disturbed' (Cronin 1991), then a delightful picture emerges of the true character of this little mouse.

Long-tailed Mice are versatile and adaptable and found in a wide range of habitats and ecotones across Tasmania. In western Tasmania they prefer wet forest and rainforest dominated by Beech *Nothofagus cunninghamii*, but in the eastern parts of the state they live in scree slopes, boulder fields and dry forest gullies. They are mainly active at night but sometimes will forage during the day, especially in winter, when the lush forest understorey buffers them against the rain and snow. The species is recognisable by its bi-coloured tail, dark on the top and white underneath, which it holds in a distinctive high curve above the body.

Placid, curious and highly sociable, they have a small home range and form permanent breeding pairs, sharing a nest with their offspring. The young are lightly furred at birth and have inward-sloping incisors that enable them to hold fast to the mother in case she is disturbed. The female plugs the entrance to the nest when she leaves to forage nearby on mosses, seeds and fungi. The young are weaned by about thirty-three days of age and they live about eighteen months to two years.

The Long-tailed Mouse is Tasmania's only endemic rodent and at present its habitat is well reserved, widespread and secure in status. It is probably one of the least known, least loved but most successful of Tasmania's native species; attributes that it shares with rodents worldwide.

TASMANIAN & KING ISLAND EMUS

Dromaius novaehollandiae diemenensis & Dromaius ater

Emus became popular soon after Europeans arrived in Van Diemen's Land, as a welcome relief from salt-beef and pork. Sadly, little remains of either the Tasmanian Emu or the King Island Emu as both were hunted to extinction before much scientific information could be gathered (Legge 1907). While all species of emu are similar in appearance, the Tasmanian Emu and King Island Emu were both smaller and darker than the mainland forms. The Tasmanian Emu was an endemic subspecies with an ashen-grey body and a whitish throat. The King Island Emu, sometimes called the black or dwarf emu, was smaller and darker again and although few descriptions of its appearance exist, its plumage was said to be black with a tinge of blue.

The King Island Emu was unique to King Island in western Bass Strait, where it once occurred in great numbers along the shores and near shady lagoons. The crew of the *Lady Nelson* first noted them in 1802, and later that year, when a French expedition arrived, the species was already being hunted for food. Delayed by bad weather, François Péron aboard *Le Géographe* recorded seeing some emus hanging on butchers' hooks, and during conversation was told each weighed 45 to 50 pounds (about 23 kg). They were being killed for food by sealers who used dogs specially trained for the purpose, and one sealer named Cowper apparently boasted of killing 300 birds himself (Brasil 1914). Péron captured several birds to take back to France and despite some dying on the way, two live birds were presented to the Empress Josephine, wife of Napoleon I. One of these birds survived until 1822, and as there are no other records of live emus on King Island after about 1805, this may have been the last of its kind (Fuller 2000).

Tasmanian Emus lived in grassland and open woodland near abundant fresh water. They reportedly ranged throughout the Midlands, in the northeast and across the northwest coastal plains. One day in 1827 Henry Hellyer, the chief surveyor for the Van Diemen's Land Company, came across a small flock while working on the northwest coast. He was so surprised and delighted he named the site Emu Bay (now Burnie). Emus were sighted regularly around New Norfolk, Mona Vale and the Avoca–Fingal district, and were frequently seen on Kearney's Bog, an upland moor near Lake Leake. In the 1840s, a Mr Ransom remembered hunting emus with kangaroo dogs when he was about eighteen years of age. He recalled the time when Captain Hepburn of Roys Hills found a nest with eight or nine eggs, which he hatched under a turkey hen. He gave a pair of these young ones to Baron von Steiglitz, of Killymoon, one of which survived until 1873 before drowning while trying to cross a flooded river (the *Mercury* 1974).

The fate of the Tasmanian Emu was to provide food for the growing colony and its naturally low numbers could never sustain the onslaught. Hunting parties were sent into the bush to 'secure native meats', which were rationed by the Public Store when 'proper' food was scarce. Proper food was always scarce. Colonel Collins assigned Hugh Germain, a private in the Marines, to hunt emu and kangaroo which, at 1 shilling 6 pence per pound, returned on average 1000 pounds per month (Dove 1926). Adults, chicks and eggs were eaten, the skins were turned into mats, the green eggs were decorated for private collections and the beautiful wispy feathers were in demand for bedding and as adornments for ladies' hats. Nothing was wasted.

So useful were emus that by the 1850s farmers such as James Cox of Clarendon, near Evandale, began keeping them under semi-domestication. As Tasmanian birds became hard and harder to find, stock was imported, mostly from Port Phillip in Victoria, though some came from elsewhere. Captive-bred Tasmanian Emus had eventually died out by the early 1870s, as pure bloodlines could no longer be sourced.

The Tasmanian Emu was last recorded in the wild somewhere between 1845 and 1865. 'Very few individuals can now exist in the island, and it is to be feared that its total extinction will be effected ere it can be ascertained whether the Tasmanian bird is identical with that of New Holland' (West 1852). West was correct; the species went extinct before it could be formally described and even today its unique taxonomic features are unknown.

In 1968, the government obtained two pairs of emus from the Melbourne Zoo and introduced them to Maria Island, off Tasmania's east coast. They were confined in a native life enclosure near Darlington in an experiment to re-create the Tasmanian subspecies through inbreeding and trait selection. One pair died within two years of their introduction but by 1976 the second pair had increased to seven adults and seventeen chicks. Although the offspring showed some characteristics of the extinct Tasmanian form, the experiment ultimately failed and in later years the birds became better known for their ability to terrorise the island's visitors.

Little survives of the King Island Emu other than bone fragments and a skin given by Baudin to the Museum of Natural History in Paris. A complete skeleton of the Tasmanian Emu was discovered in a cave at Mole Creek in 1974, and is housed at the Queen Victoria Museum, Launceston. One egg and two skins (male and female) of the Tasmanian Emu are held in the Natural History Museum in London, having been sent there in 1837 by Ronald Campbell Gunn (Green 1960, Macdonald 1962). In 2005, an art dealer in Hobart put up a single Tasmanian Emu egg for auction; apparently it had been collected in the 1850s near Gould's Country and was complete with embryo. It had a reserve of $30,000 but did not sell.

ROYAL PENGUIN

Eudyptes schlegeli

Penguins worldwide have a delightful whimsical charm and the Royal Penguin is no exception. Comical, stoic and seemingly carefree, this species is superbly adapted to the marine environment and is a skilful predator in the seas around Macquarie Island.

Macquarie Island is a place like no other. About 1500 km south-southeast of Tasmania, the island is a mere speck in the Southern Ocean. The temperatures are cold and the wind relentless, just perfect for the Royal Penguin, which stands no more than 75 cm high and weighs 6 kg (Marchant & Higgins 1990). The sight of a penguin colony is overwhelming – thousands and thousands of dots, each dot becoming a bird, each bird moving on its tiny patch, the massive colony singing and pulsating with life. The colony is ordered yet in continual motion. With head bobbing, wings flapping, squabbling and shuffling, every bird goes about its daily routine, most of which is centred around breeding.

Royal Penguins mature by about ten years of age and from then on they begin their journey back to the island each year to breed. They start this ritual by building or refurbishing their modest nest with rocks, collected nearby or stolen from neighbours. The first egg is laid by October but is rarely incubated and usually abandoned. The second and slightly larger egg is more precious and is carefully balanced on the top of the feet, each parent taking weekly shifts to keep it warm until it hatches. The chick is lovingly nurtured and by three weeks of age is covered in down and large enough to spend time in a community crèche. The chicks are fully feathered by the end of January, and by February have left the island and are foraging far out to sea (Marchant & Higgins 1990).

On land they may appear clumsy, but in water Royal Penguins are graceful and swift. They are streamlined and acrobatic and hunt by hot pursuit, capturing krill and small fish while diving and darting in every direction. As they toboggan ashore their yellow wispy crest falls about their face and their bright pink feet flap beneath the sheen of their formal 'dinner suit'.

Life for the Royal Penguin was not always this carefree. In 1887, after Joseph Hatch & Co. from New Zealand had devastated the island's seal populations, they turned their attention to penguins. 'As many as 2,000 birds can be put through the digesters in a day, equal to 14 casks of oil, each about 40 gallons … the penguins can be easily driven and yarded like sheep. When the yard is full, 10 men go out and club the birds before breakfast … when work is resumed many of the poor birds are found to have recovered … and require reclubbing' (Cumpston 1968). This slaughter continued for nearly thirty years because Hatch, a gifted speaker and politician, convinced authorities that the industry was acceptable and sustainable. As opposition to the slaughter grew, Hatch relocated his business headquarters to Hobart to improve his chances of renewing the lease. But this was unsuccessful, and in 1920 the Tasmanian Government terminated his operations on Macquarie Island. Joseph Hatch died in Hobart in September 1928 and is buried in an unmarked grave at the Cornelian Bay Cemetery.

Royal Penguins have now recovered and the largest colonies at Hurd Point hold more than 500,000 breeding pairs (Terauds & Stewart 2008). Eradicating pests from the island will help maintain their breeding habitat and will aid the survival of so many other unique species that call this place home.

orange
burnt.
sienna
red

WANDERING ALBATROSS

Diomedea exulans

Albatrosses are the largest flying birds in the world and there are twenty-two species found worldwide. The genus *Diomedea* includes all the largest of the group and there are none so large or graceful as the Wandering Albatross on Tasmania's remote Macquarie Island.

Greek legend has it that Diomedes was a valiant warrior in the Trojan War and that when he died his grief-stricken companions metamorphosed into birds to follow his spirit. *Exulans* is Greek, meaning to exile or spend long periods away, and this very accurately describes a species that can be at sea for up to seven years before returning home to breed.

Albatrosses pair for life and this strong mate fidelity builds the commitment necessary to raise a single chick over the long winter months. Every breeding season, pairs renew their devotion with a spectacular courtship display. This ritual consists of bowing, wing flapping, calling skyward and an elegant dip of the bill beneath the wing followed by bouts of mutual preening, dancing and duets of ecstasy, ending with a groan and a yap (Jouventin & Lequette 1990).

A single egg is laid in a conical nest, little more than a mound of earth. About eleven weeks later it hatches and the chick is nurtured daily for the next month or so. After it has grown a thick coat of down, the parents feed it less frequently and over the next eight or nine months the chick spends increasingly long, lonely periods awaiting their return. By the end of the rearing period, albatross chicks have consumed close to 100 kg of food and are certainly ready in size and strength to leave the nest (Marchant & Higgins 1990).

Wandering Albatross breed in large numbers on many islands in the sub-Antarctic and it is only the Macquarie Island population that is perilously close to extinction. Thought to have once numbered about 200 breeding pairs, the population began to decline soon after sealers arrived on the island and by the early 1900s it was reduced to just a handful of birds (Terauds *et al.* 2006). They were seldom seen by Douglas Mawson's scientific crew, stationed on the island from 1911 to 1913, though one memorable story exists. One day while Hutchinson and Hurley were retrieving a camera lens left at Caroline Cove, they came across a bird sitting on a grassy slope. In Mawson's (1934) words, they could not resist the impulse to secure it for the collection and despite having neither firearm nor crossbow, the resourceful Hurley was able to throw a tin of preserved meat and hit it on the head.

Where once the remoteness of Macquarie Island protected the population from decline, longline fishing vessels have now expanded into every part of the world's oceans. Albatrosses and other seabirds have learned to follow fishing boats and as they scavenge baits from the longline hooks, they are dragged under the water and drown. Millions of hooks are set annually worldwide and even though only a small percentage of albatrosses are killed, the potential exists to bring nearly every species to the point of extinction.

While there are international treaties and agreements governing the global management of albatrosses, it remains an ongoing challenge. Scientists in Tasmania have been at the forefront of this species' conservation for years by continuing long-term monitoring programs and designing deployment equipment to help reduce the albatross bycatch. Next time you eat deep-sea fish, think of the Wanderer's dance and their calling skyward to yap.

WEDGE-TAILED EAGLE

Aquila audax fleayi

'To rise from the ground it runs or hops for a few metres and with slow, heavy wing-beats soon becomes air-borne. By flying into the wind and taking full advantage of up-draughts, it can quickly ascend to a great height, spiralling on outstretched wings with rarely a beat.' (Green 1995)

Tasmania's subspecies of Wedge-tailed Eagle has been isolated for thousands of years, due to its reluctance to cross open water. Like many island forms, it has become larger and darker than those on mainland Australia, but like eagles worldwide, it is a powerful and superbly designed hunting and killing machine.

The wings of the Wedge-tailed Eagle are long and broad for soaring over land. The primary feathers are notched and when outstretched interlock to form 'fingers' which reduce drag and give extra lift. During flight, the wedge-shaped tail provides extra surface area and can be either fanned or narrowed, according to need. For seizing and ripping, the eagle has deeply curved talons and a massive bill, but it's also a scavenger, and its partly bare face is an adaptation for feeding on carrion. Even the bird's dark colour is due to heavier pigment in the feathers, which enhances their strength and durability (Olsen 1995).

Despite their size and formidable appearance, Wedge-tailed Eagles are a shy nesting species and are easily disturbed while breeding. Nest trees are carefully chosen in a large patch of forest and are often mid-slope in a sheltered gully. Massive stick nests are built to withstand climatic extremes and many nests survive for centuries. Even though eagles may have three or more nests in their territory, only one is used each season. During breeding, from August to January, the male bird performs a spectacular 'pot hook' courtship display and with folded wings and fanned tail plummets downwards for 70 metres or so, followed by an upswing. While two eggs are normally laid, the larger chick usually kills the smaller, younger one a few days after hatching. This practice, known as siblicide, is common in large birds of prey and although seemingly wasteful, it promotes survival of the fittest (Olsen 1995). By one month of age the chick is downy white with a striking black beak and feisty disposition. As it grows, it treads clumsily around the nest, bobbing, nodding and flapping precariously near the edge. Young eaglets are tawny brown with a blonde nape but darken as they mature and are almost black by twenty years of age. Eagles can live up to thirty or so years in the wild, but one bird, formerly displayed at Woodville Zoo at Granton, reached forty-seven years of age, though by then it was looking a little 'weary' (Bill Brown pers. comm.).

Eagles play a critical role in the environment as they kill the sick and the weak and clean up the carcases. Since the loss of the Thylacine and now the decline of the Tasmanian Devil, never before has their role been more critical. Sadly, ever-diminishing forests, collision and electrocution on powerlines and even eco-developments such as wind farms continue to cause an impact, and now this species is threatened with extinction (Threatened Species Section 2006a). Private properties with eagle nests are now being targeted for conservation protection with financial incentives offered to covenant or sell. The traditional protection zone of 10 ha around a nest is no longer considered adequate to protect the eagle's privacy, so larger buffers are being sought.

TASMANIAN NATIVE-HEN

Gallinula mortierii

The Tasmanian Native-hen is a special bird in every respect. Not only does it have a fascinating way of life but its fossil history dates back to the Pleistocene to a species that has changed little since the last ice age.

About 26,000 years ago the ancestral form of the Tasmanian Native-hen *Tribonyx mortierii* occurred throughout Queensland, Victoria and South Australia. Its distribution followed the Murray–Darling catchment as the species favoured lush, wet areas where it grazed upon herbaceous lawns kept short by browsing marsupials (Baird 1984). Over time, as the climate became hotter, these wet areas dried out, forcing *Tribonyx* to move further south, where it eventually crossed over the Bassian land bridge and into Tasmania. Fossil bones found at Montagu in northwest Tasmania and Beginners Luck Cave in the Florentine Valley date back to the Pleistocene period, confirming that the species has been on this island for a very long time (Van Tets 1978). When the land bridge flooded about 12,000 years ago, the birds on mainland Australia faced increasing predation pressure and spiralled to extinction, whereas the population now isolated in Tasmania expanded and flourished.

Little has changed since prehistoric times. The life of the Tasmanian Native-hen is still governed by water, which in turn regulates its food availability and life cycle. However, the species has capitalised on modified habitats and has successfully expanded its range by using farmland, paddocks and even roadside verges.

Native-hens are a deep slate grey colour blending to russet brown on their lower portions, with stunning red eyes that offset their yellow bill. Although they are flightless, their wings are neither vestigial nor rudimentary, but large and deeply curved. While they are good swimmers, their real talent is for running and when pushed they can reach speeds of up to 50 km per hour using their outstretched wings for balance and manoeuvrability (Marchant & Higgins 1993).

Life for the 'bush chook' has been described as one of love, passion, loss and drama (Apthorp 1992) as they have an unusual social structure, called 'cooperative polyandry', which is rare in the animal kingdom. Family groups comprise one dominant female and several subordinate male helpers who take on the role of raising the chicks. Keeping the rabble together requires constant work and there is much gesturing, calling, tail flicking and running about. Territorial boundaries are tight and seldom crossed unless covertly; if intruders are detected, vigorous sparring matches break out. Their alarm call has the distinctive note of a crosscut saw and in a sudden burst of ecstasy a chorus erupts with perfect alternation, the males producing the higher-pitched note (Marchant & Higgins 1993).

Native-hens build two types of nests – one for egg laying and the other to brood their young. Newborn chicks are black fluff-balls with tiny arm-like wings and legs strong enough to run alongside the adults. The large white dot at the end of their beak keeps them visible in the long grass.

After centuries of being considered little more than a pasture pest, the Tasmanian Native-hen finally gained legal protection in 2007, and this only came about after tireless lobbying by the volunteer ornithological group Birds Tasmania. The species is now recognised as an important part of Tasmania's avifauna and can be more fully appreciated for its uniqueness in the ornithological world. Ironically, once again the 'narky' faces the pressure of a changing climate as the land dries out, as well as a potential new predator, the fox – but unlike in the past, it has nowhere left to run.

SWIFT PARROT

Lathamus discolor

Once described as Tasmania's commonest 'lorikeet', the Swift Parrot is now nationally endangered with a population of fewer than 1000 pairs. In 2009 the government declared that this population was 'unlikely to be viable in the long term' (the *Mercury* 2009), meaning that unless more is done to protect the species, extinction is inevitable.

Swift Parrots, it seems, are prone to decline. They fly so fast they crash into things, they breed in tree hollows that are rapidly disappearing, and they rely on a food source that is highly variable in any given season. To make matters worse, they migrate. In fact, Swift Parrots fly the longest distance of any parrot in the world, and that's very risky behaviour (SPRT 2008). Every year around late April, Swift Parrots fly to the mainland to replenish their energy reserves over winter. They travel across Victoria, up into northern New South Wales and sometimes even as far north as Queensland, foraging in box–ironbark woodland and dry eucalypt forest along the way.

By August, Swift Parrots begin returning to Tasmania to breed. They fly down the east coast to St Helens then disperse as far south as Recherche Bay, although a few birds – possibly remnants of a once more widespread population – instinctively head west to the Gog Range area. By now, Swift Parrots have developed a voracious appetite for nectar and are frantically searching for flowering Blue Gums *Eucalyptus globulus* and Black Gums *Eucalyptus ovata*. They have a specially designed brush-tipped tongue to extract nectar from the flowers and they rely on this high-energy food to breed successfully. Eucalypt flowering is a sporadic event in Tasmania and in any given area gums will flower perhaps once in every two to four years. This means that the parrots have to search constantly for food, often flying great distances between forest patches and visiting urban gardens and parkland along the way.

During breeding, pairs choose a tree hollow well away from disturbance to raise their young. The hollow needs to be as close as possible to their food supply, as the less energy they spend on commuting, the more time they will have to tend their brood, and maybe even lay a second clutch in the season. It takes six weeks to raise their chicks and the parents fly constantly between their nest and flowering gums, one bird often standing sentinel while the chicks are being fed. By March the fledglings leave the nest and soon after this the entire Swift Parrot population begins its long journey back to the mainland, congregating in the north of the state to wait for favourable weather before crossing Bass Strait.

In the early days, trees were felled by hand using axe and crosscut saw and hauled to where the timber could be milled. Nowadays thousands of hectares of native forest can be cleared in a year and the ground made ready to replant more. But trees are like red wine – they improve with age, and it takes hundreds of years to form a tree hollow suitable for a parrot to breed in. Since European settlement, more than half of the original grassy Blue Gum forest of eastern Tasmania has been cleared (Brereton *et al.* 2004), and even now patches critical for Swift Parrot survival, like those at Wielangta, are being fragmented and lost.

Swift Parrots are joyous birds with a carefree charm, and their feathers shine iridescent as they race from tree to tree. Sadly, it seems that their forests and population both decline while we continually talk about how to save them.

80% Y
20% B

95% Y
5% B

Red forehead

Deep blue
cheeks + throat

2R
1Y
1B

90% Y
5% R
5% B

95% Y
5% B

100% Y

100% B

100% R

60% R
40% Y

40% R
60% Y

50% R
40% Y
10% B

GREEN ROSELLA

Platycercus caledonicus

'… soon after the establishment of the colonies of Van Diemen's Land, pies made of the bird here represented were commonly eaten at every table. It was not long after my arrival in the country before I tested the goodness of the flesh of this bird as a viand, and I found it so excellent that I partook of it whenever an opportunity for my doing so presented itself.' (Gould 1848)

Apparently, Mrs Beeton's recipe, upon which these pies were based, required twelve small parakeets of the tropical kind, trussed up like quail, placed above beef, bacon, eggs and parsley, with a cooking time of about two hours. Chances are that six Green Rosellas would have sufficed.

The first specimens of Green Rosella were collected from Adventure Bay on Bruny Island in January 1777, during Captain Cook's third and final voyage to Australia. They were obtained by the surgeon William Anderson and beautifully painted by William Ellis, the surgeon's mate. Years later, in reference to Anderson's diaries, the British ornithologist John Latham erroneously reported their type locality as being New Caledonia. When this account was formally transcribed by the German scientist Johann Friedrich Gmelin, he immortalised the species name as *caledonicus*. Mistakes such as this were commonplace, as it must have been difficult enough to prepare specimens at sea, let alone remember where they had been collected.

Surprisingly few scientific studies have been made of Tasmania's Green Rosella. They begin breeding in their second year and, like most other parrot and cockatoo species, probably pair for life. They require tree hollows for nesting, but if these are in short supply they will sometimes use other crevices, such as wall or roof cavities; this behaviour is particularly common on King Island, where large trees are scarce.

Breeding starts in early spring with pairs becoming secretive so as not to disclose the nest site. Their courtship ritual is full of chatter and promise and as the male approaches the female he squares his shoulders, drops his wings, puffs his chest and vigorously wags his tail from side to side (Higgins 1999). Adults prepare the nest by first chipping and moulding the entrance, then once inside, they scrape the floor to line it with wood dust. Four to five eggs are laid on consecutive days and both adults help to raise the young.

The species' movements are poorly known and although the birds are capable of sustained flight, they are relatively sedentary and travel only short distances. 'When the nesting season is over it resorts to cultivated land, orchards and gardens. It has a neat way of holding tiny potatoes or artichokes in one claw while it balances on the other. But parrots are wasteful eaters and seem to throw down more than half of what they planned to enjoy' (Fletcher 1956). Small flocks of six to eight birds share communal roosts during the winter and often congregate in paddocks or along roads to feed on rosehip, blackberry or other weed species. They also take small pieces of grit from the roadside verge, to maintain the grinding function of their gizzard, but if disturbed, they will rise gracefully, calling *cossick cossick*, as they glide to the forest edge.

ORANGE-BELLIED PARROT

Neophema chrysogaster

Deny King's vegetable garden at Melaleuca in Port Davey was filled with a curious mix of wild, edible and not-so-edible plants. Every spring he turned the soil and as he did, down they would come: Green Rosellas, Grey Shrike-thrushes and Orange-bellied Parrots. He had been gardening like this for years and what he couldn't eat, the birds did. Few people realised just how important Deny's garden was until the Orange-bellied Parrot became known as one of the most endangered birds in the world.

The first specimen of an Orange-bellied Parrot was collected in 1787 during Captain Cook's visit to Adventure Bay on Bruny Island. The bird soon became known as a migratory species, spending its winter on the mainland of Australia, then returning to Tasmania to breed. In the 1830s, small flocks were flushed on the Actaeon Islands near Southport and birds were recorded breeding at Bothwell and at Melton Mowbray in Tasmania's Midlands. On the mainland, Orange-bellied Parrots were reportedly in their 'thousands' along the coast from Adelaide to Sydney and were frequently shot or captured for the aviculture trade (Brown & Wilson 1982). A spate of records between 1880 and the early 1900s suggests that the species was numerous and locally common.

What happened to the species after this period is uncertain; however, by the 1970s the population had dramatically declined and by the 1980s it numbered just a few hundred individuals. It seemed that apart from the handful of birds visiting Deny's garden, 'it is possible that the total population of the Orange-bellied Parrot is now at so low a level … it will be necessary to take the decision either to allow it to slide into eventual extinction, or to undertake a captive breeding program' (Brown & Wilson 1980). This sentiment set alarm bells ringing and a national recovery program was immediately launched, supported financially by federal and state governments and other interested parties.

This recovery program continues today and is one of the longest running of any in the world. The program involves a range of conservation measures such as captive breeding for release, adaptive field management and habitat modelling to better understand the species' ecology. Custom-built nest boxes have been erected in Tasmania's southwest forests and these are monitored yearly for breeding success. About fifty pairs of birds are held in aviaries around southeast Australia and the captive-bred juveniles are released each year to help boost the population (J. Long pers. comm.). Nearly every bird is individually banded and every year volunteers monitor research sites at Melaleuca and Birchs Inlet, or along the Victorian coast, recording the arrival and activity of birds throughout the season.

In late February to March, adult Orange-bellied Parrots begin their long migration back to the mainland, with juveniles following about a month later. They travel up Tasmania's west coast, fossicking along the deserted beaches or in the buttongrass plains as they go. Before crossing Bass Strait they stop briefly on islands dotted around the Hunter Group, foraging on saltmarsh, wetlands or paddock weeds.

The total population of Orange-bellied Parrots is still fewer than 200 birds, and despite best efforts, it seems impossible to increase this figure. However, there is no quick fix to the decline of a threatened species and invariably we are in for the long haul. Recovery programs are complex and challenging. They involve our limited knowledge of the species' ecology, the continual demand to modify its environment and a chronic lack of money to fund what is needed. Ultimately, success relies on those who believe that the Orange-bellied Parrot, like so many other species, deserves to survive in the wild, no matter how long it takes.

AUSTRALIA

NEW ZEALAND

TASMANIA

MACQUARIE ISLAND

ANTARCTICA

MACQUARIE ISLAND PARAKEET & RAIL

Cyanoramphus novaezelandiae erythrotis & Gallirallus philippensis macquariensis

By the turn of the nineteenth century, oil was increasingly in demand for lighting, heating and all manner of modern-day comforts. Whaling and sealing operations now turned their attention towards the untapped islands of the Arctic and sub-Antarctic. In October 1807, a Sydney merchant called Robert Campbell contracted Frederick Hasselburg, master of the brig *Perseverance*, to sail forth and procure oil, skins and any other useful animal substances. Hasselburg sighted Macquarie Island on 11 July 1810 and named it after the Governor of New South Wales, Lachlan Macquarie. Upon landing there, the crew eagerly disembarked and commenced procurement.

Lying midway between Tasmania and Antarctica, Macquarie Island is about 34 km long and dominated by a massive plateau that drops away to steep, rugged escarpments. The slopes are carpeted with tussock grassland, herbfield and lush Macquarie Island Cabbage *Stilbocarpa polaris* and wallows and peat bogs up to 6 m deep occur on the raised beach terraces and flatter inland areas.

The Macquarie Island Parakeet and Macquarie Island Rail once lived on this remote island, both having radiated there from ancestral families that are still quite widespread today. The Macquarie Island Parakeet was a subspecies of the Red-crowned Parakeet or Kakariki *Cyanoramphus novaezelandiae*, commonly found throughout New Zealand, Norfolk Island and New Caledonia. The Macquarie Island Rail was an endemic subspecies of the Buff-banded Rail *Gallirallus philippensis* still found in Tasmania (though rare), mainland Australia and the southwestern Pacific region.

The Macquarie Island Parakeet was about 28 cm long and a beautiful emerald green colour with a crimson forehead and patch behind the eye. As there are no trees on Macquarie Island, they nested either in a burrow they excavated deep underground or in a well-concealed nest built in dense, matted tussock or fern. They ate seeds, fruits and invertebrates and were often observed picking among the seaweed on the rocky coastline.

Men living on the island at the time often killed and ate parakeets to relieve their monotonous diet, or kept them as pets, and some were even sold at the bird markets of Sydney, as apparently they were 'good talkers' (Taylor 1979). In 1820, Captain Thaddeus Bellingshausen of the Russian Antarctic Expedition purchased a single live bird for three bottles of rum and collected another twenty specimens to send to museums in Europe. Macquarie Island Parakeets were apparently still plentiful in 1877 when Thomson and his shipwrecked companions wrote, 'we shot and roasted two brace of small green parakeets … and occasionally we were successful in knocking them over with stones … there appeared to be great numbers of them.' (Cumpston 1968)

The Macquarie Island Rail was about 21 cm in length and handsomely banded in chestnut, black and white with a reddish-brown tail that flicked nervously when it walked. A shy bird, it was rarely seen and although it could fly, it seldom did, preferring instead to forage in grassy areas for snails, insects and other bits and pieces.

For the first seventy years or so after the island's discovery, the Macquarie Island Parakeet and Macquarie Island Rail remained widespread and abundant. However, records show that after about 1880 both species had become increasingly rare and by 1894 were, in fact, extinct. Something had changed on the island to tip the ecological balance.

From the moment humans stepped ashore on Macquarie Island, exotic pests came with them. At one time dogs ran wild and feral cats steadily built up in number. In 1872, Weka, a flightless Maori hen, were deliberately released on the island as a food source to safeguard against starvation. They were slow to establish, so a second release was made in 1879 along with a French strain of rabbit. The rabbits were purchased in Dunedin by Elder and Co. and less than two years after being released at North East Bay were reported to be 'swarming' over the island (Cumpston 1968).

After spending more than three years on Macquarie Island (1896 to 1900) collecting specimens for the Colonial Museum in Wellington, the taxidermist Joseph R. Burton wrote, 'Formerly there existed on Macquarie a small parakeet and a rail peculiar to the island. Probably they are now extinct because I hunted high and low without seeing any trace of them. The wild domestic cats that were brought over, or were shipwrecked on the island, and that now prowl over the place, may be the cause of the regrettable disappearance of these interesting birds.' (Cumpston 1968)

Burton was partly correct, as cats certainly were having an impact; however, it was the explosion in rabbit numbers that had tipped the ecological balance. Prior to rabbits being released, an equilibrium had formed between exotic pests and native food supply. Suddenly, more rabbits meant more food for cats and for scavenging Weka, and consequently cat and Weka numbers exploded. Rabbits in turn consumed the vegetation, exposing the nest sites of the rail and parakeet to even greater predation pressures. In November 1901, while en route to the Antarctic, a small crew from

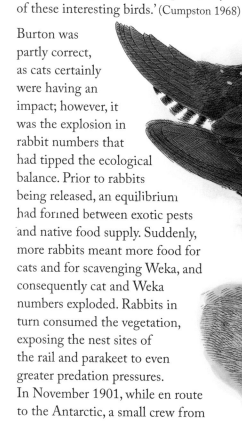

Captain Scott's
Discovery Expedition
came ashore for a few
hours' collecting. No parakeets
or rails were to be seen and even though
the zoologist Edward Wilson collected many
specimens of what he termed 'Rothschild's Landrail',
these were supposedly Weka.

In less than a hundred years since Macquarie Island was discovered, more than 250,000 seals and penguins had been rendered for oil and more than 200,000 skins had been exported for use as clothing and in other domestic products (Cumpston 1968). One seal species (an undescribed upland seal) had been exterminated and the remaining seal and penguin populations were on the verge of total collapse. In 1915, Sir Douglas Mawson started a campaign to end the harvesting industry and as support for his campaign grew, so did the public's abhorrence of the cruel slaughter of wildlife. But it took eighteen long years before the battle was finally won. On 17 May 1933, Sir Hubert Nicholls, Lieutenant-Governor of Tasmania, signed a proclamation declaring Macquarie Island a wildlife sanctuary. While this proclamation may have saved the seal and penguin populations, sadly the Macquarie Island Parakeet and Macquarie Island Rail were long gone; they had slipped to extinction before many had even noticed.

Macquarie Island's wildlife has slowly recovered and today restoration of the island's ecosystem is a conservation priority. Wekas were eradicated by 1988 and after twenty years of hard work, the last feral cat, a female, was shot at Sawyer Creek near Green Gorge in June 2000. An integrated pest eradication program to finally rid the island of rabbits, rats and mice is now under way, representing another exciting chapter in this amazing island's history.

MASKED OWL

Tyto novaehollandiae castanops

'Van Diemen's Land is the native country of this Owl … few of the Raptorial birds, in fact, with the exception of the Eagles, are more formidable or more sanguinary in disposition … The sexes differ very considerably in size, the female being by far the largest, and in every way more powerful than the male: the stroke of her foot and the grasp of her talons must be immediate death to any animal.' (Gould 1848)

How right John Gould was, for in addition to being hypnotically beautiful, the Tasmanian subspecies of Masked Owl is superbly designed to catch and kill.

The Masked Owl has a simple hunting technique – it flies, perches and waits until something passes nearby. Using its strong, muscular neck, it rotates the head to scan for any movement on the ground, and its black, round eyes are centrally placed, with a transfixing and haunting stare. Its heart-shaped facial disk is lined with a fine black ruff of partly erectile feathers and this entire configuration acts like a parabola by channelling light and sound to the eyes and ears. The owl's chestnut-flecked body feathers have the quality of eiderdown, providing warmth without weight and being amazingly soft to the touch. The webbing of the outer flight feathers has a short, comb-like fringe that muffles the flow of air over the wingtips. This suite of features enables the owl to hunt in almost total darkness by being able to see and hear its prey, then swoop without making a sound.

But Masked Owls can make a big impression when they want to. In the dead of night their harsh, high-pitched screech can be heard across the valley as birds call to signal their territory. If agitated, they will hunch over and sway from side to side, clacking their beak, hissing and screaming, or if brought to the ground, they assume a defence posture by leaning on their back and brandishing their strongly curved talons as weapons.

The short breeding season extends from late October to early November, and pairs need a large tree hollow for nesting. Nest hollows can be either in a large patch of forest or sometimes just an old tree in an open paddock. Two to three eggs are laid and when hatched the young are constantly brooded by the female for the first few weeks until their eyes are open. As the chicks continue to grow, both adults take on hunting for food, and will sometimes drop pieces of rabbit or rat into the hollow while flying past (Higgins 1999). When they are about seven weeks of age and have grown their pinfeathers, the chicks can sometimes be seen peering from the nest hollow awaiting their parents' return.

Masked Owls have well-spaced territories of up to 1000 ha in area and studies have shown that they prefer dry sclerophyll forest and woodland or cleared land mosaics with forest edges (Mooney 1997). These habitats offer an abundance of small mammals, especially rodents and rabbits, and sometimes other birds are preyed upon. As the female Masked Owl is significantly larger than the male, she also hunts possum and wallaby, and anything that can't be digested is disgorged in a huge pellet tightly bound by bone and fur.

Tasmania's Masked Owl is now threatened with extinction. Its reliance on old trees for nesting means these are where we must focus our conservation efforts.

really light wash of yellow laid down first, then diluted black added to yellow to make olive-green ● - then worked over yellow in layers to build colour - colour worked over with fine pen to and indicate form and feather texture.

FORTY-SPOTTED PARDALOTE

Pardalotus quadragintus

One of the first scenes of Hobart Town is a painting by George Prideaux Harris from 1806. In the background is Hunter Island, where the settlement of Hobart first began, and in the foreground a pair of pardalotes sits above the stump of a newly felled tree. Ironically, two centuries later, the survival of Tasmania's endemic Forty-spotted Pardalote depends on the sentiment of this very scene.

There are three species of pardalote in Tasmania: the Spotted Pardalote *Pardalotus punctatus*, Striated Pardalote *P. striatus* and Forty-spotted Pardalote *P. quadragintus*. All are commonly called diamond birds because of their exquisite, jewel-like appearance. Gould (1848) likened them to the 'tits of Europe, creeping and clinging among the branches in every direction' and this very accurately describes their behaviour. Rather than see them, you are more likely to hear the plaintive *where where* call of Forty-spotted Pardalotes as they feed high in the eucalypts, using a small notch on the end of their bill to gather insects, lerp and sugary manna.

They nest mostly in tree cavities or sometimes use fallen limbs, old fence posts or a hole in the ground. The breeding season is from August to January, with a second clutch laid if the first one is lost (Higgins & Peter 2002). 'Their little white eggs were once much sought for by professional collectors, but their nests were extremely hard to find' (Sharland 1971). Both adults help raise the chicks and every time they return to the nest, they settle close by, waiting to hear the chicks' whirring sound before diving down to the entrance with a beak full of food. By twenty-three days of age, the chicks are fully feathered and ready to fly. They scramble to the top of the nest, stretch their legs, spread their tiny wings and off they go.

Historically, the Forty-spotted Pardalote occurred from Flinders Island to Recherche Bay and occasionally at The Steppes, Bothwell and possibly even on King Island (Littler 1910). Gould (1848) described them as abundant in the gullies under Mount Wellington, where he collected a 'perfectly developed white egg from the body of a female'. By the 1980s the species' range had declined to a few offshore islands and the headland of Tinderbox Peninsula, and totalled just a few thousand birds (Threatened Species Section 2006b). This decline was due to loss of habitat and increasing competition, for whenever there is disturbance, larger, more aggressive birds move in. Forty-spotted Pardalotes are sedentary and territorial and adults seldom fly far from their colony. They depend on one type of tree, the White Gum *Eucalyptus viminalis*, and this alone is critical to their survival. White Gums provide their food, shelter and occasionally their nesting sites, and are fundamental to their colony. Even though the conservation message is simple – don't cut their White Gums down – as industry and housing expand, colonies continue to be lost.

In 1991, Ross and Josephine Denne decided that their piece of bush on Bruny Island was too important to subdivide and donated 92 ha for the species' protection. In 1995, when the Dennes Hill Nature Reserve was proclaimed, it was the first time the government and private landholders had joined together to protect habitat for a nationally endangered species. Years later, the residents on Bruny Island are following the Dennes' lead by covenanting their White Gums and planting more where needed. While still at risk of extinction, this wonderful little bird is holding fast to its tiny patch of bush and may just survive as we expand our efforts.

tiny small notch or overhang at tip of bill

front view of open bill

side view of bill showing notch at tip

TASMANIAN THORNBILL & SCRUBTIT

Acanthiza ewingii & Acanthornis magnus

From the moment John Gould stepped ashore at Hobart Town in 1838, his intention was to collect as many bird specimens as possible. During his five-month visit, the fruits of his labours were three nine-gallon kegs of specimens in spirits, 500 bird skins, 100 skeletons, sixty nests with eggs, and assigning names to seven of Tasmania's endemic species. Two species of which Gould made particular mention were Ewings Thornbill and the Scrubtit; this is quite surprising given both are small brown birds, with seemingly unremarkable ways of life.

Before Gould had even arrived in Australia he speculated, correctly, that there were probably two closely aligned thornbills living in Tasmania's forests. The first he called the Tasmanian Thornbill *Acanthiza diemenensis*, and the second Ewings Thornbill *Acanthiza ewingi*, after his colleague and friend the Reverend Thomas J. Ewing, chaplain and headmaster of the Queen's Orphan School. Ewings Thornbills prefer higher-altitude forests and fern gullies and live either singly, in pairs or with other small forest birds, calling with a sweet babbling song as they dance amid the foliage foraging for insects. Their nests are often parasitised by cuckoos, who evict the eggs of the host and deposit their own, resulting in an enormous chick being raised by tiny thornbill parents.

Gould unwittingly created all sorts of confusion about these two Tasmanian thornbill species. Firstly, Richter's painting in 1848 did not accentuate their major field difference, namely the Ewings' fluffy white undertail-coverts. Gould himself failed to emphasise their differences in his Handbook published in 1865, and then omitted Ewings Thornbill altogether from his catalogue for the British Museum. A result of this oversight was that the Ewings Thornbill was forgotten for the next forty years. Imagine the excitement when in 1903, during the Royal Australian Ornithologists Union congress, a live specimen was obtained from the slopes of Mount Wellington and exhibited 'in the flesh' (Littler 1910). To further confuse this story, after Ewings Thornbill was quickly reinstated to Australia's list of birds, it was renamed the Tasmanian Thornbill, as it was endemic to this island, whereas the Tasmanian Thornbill was renamed the Brown Thornbill, as it was synonymous with the species found across southeastern Australia.

Gould did not collect the Scrubtit during his visit to Van Diemen's Land but described the species from a study skin sent to him in 1855 by Ronald C. Gunn. Gould knew the species was both distinct from yet somehow closely related to the Thornbills *Acanthiza* and the Scrubwren *Sericornis*, so he called it *Acanthornis* as an amalgam of both names.

On their behaviour, a Mr Butler in 1905 remarked, 'I have spent many hours watching this bird feeding and building its nest, and to my mind it closely resembles the tree creepers (Certhiidae). With its mouse-like movements, it will fly to the base of a tree-fern, run rapidly to the top and down the other side, just pausing long enough to grasp an unwary beetle or some such small object, then off again to another tree and repeat the performance' (Littler 1910). Scrubtits breed from September to January but their ecology is poorly known. They are probably sedentary and monogamous and do not have helpers at the nest. They live in high-rainfall areas, mainly in rainforest, beech and subalpine wet forests across Tasmania. While the species' status is secure, a small remnant population in the paperbark forest of the Nook Swamp on King Island is rapidly declining due to wildfires and loss of habitat and is now in danger of extinction.

11 yellow
+ 5 orange
+ 1 burnt sienna

sepia

11 yellow
+ 1 orange

+ 4 orange

+ increasing
dilutel
black

100% orange

3 red
4 blue
2 yellow

2 red 2 blue
2 yellow

Colman's lusterdar
— straight red (cadmium)
— straight yellow (cadmium)
— straight blue (cobalt)

5 yellow + 1 red

straight yellow

YELLOW WATTLEBIRD

Anthochaera paradoxa

Tasmania's endemic Yellow Wattlebird is the largest of all Australia's honeyeaters. 'The voice of this species is most remarkable, and once heard is not easily forgotten … The cry is loud and harsh, and is between a cough and a scolding voice suffering from a cold in the throat. Its discordant nature is most in evidence when two or more birds are quarrelling' (Littler 1910). Not only is its call remarkable, but so is its timing, for the bird has an uncanny knack of calling early in the morning, and 'If one happens to be camped amidst the eucalypts when they are in flower … there will not be much chance of sleep after the first pale streak of dawn'. (Lord & Scott 1924)

Yellow Wattlebirds are streamlined and handsome birds. Both sexes have similar plumage, although the male is larger than the female, being about 50 cm in length. Despite their large size they move through the canopy with agility and ease, probing for insects and grubs and using their gently curved beak and brush-tipped tongue to extract nectar from even the tiniest flowers. During late autumn many wattlebirds migrate from the mountaintops down to woodlands and gardens where they gorge on over-ripe fruit and fill the air with their joyful chorusing and duets.

Breeding starts around August with the building of an untidy twig nest. Nests are lined with soft bits and pieces and soon become flattened under the weight and constant activity of the anxious parents. Adults become aggressive at this time of year and vigorously defend their nesting territory, bullying and swooping at all intruders. The female lays two to three purple-blotched eggs, which she incubates for sixteen days. The chicks are dutifully fed for about three weeks, by which time their flight feathers have grown and their finely streaked plumage has begun to darken.

During the early days of settlement Yellow Wattlebirds were heavily hunted and were considered the most highly esteemed of game birds. In 1839 the ornithologist John Gould remarked, 'hundreds are annually sent to the markets of Hobart Town for the purpose of the table', and apparently they were tastiest after fattening on the nectar of late-flowering eucalypts. Such was the scale of the slaughter that at one stage concerns were raised the species might go extinct. In 1902 a decision was made to temporarily close the season to afford the species two years of absolute protection (Littler 1910). Yellow Wattlebirds soon recovered in numbers and as the hunting continued, one farmer recalled that during the 1950s, 'you could go out in a party and get 150–160 or more, bring them home … hang them for a week in the cellar … pluck them and after that boil them up for about 6–7 hours … When I first got married my wife said they were ready after 3 hours but we couldn't eat them. We learnt!' (Midlands Bushweb 2003). Requests to shoot Yellow Wattlebirds were still being made into the 1970s, but tastes had changed and the Tasmanian Government closed the May 'open season' soon after. They are now protected, and killing them carries a fine. Unfortunately, a distinct subspecies of Yellow Wattlebird on King Island has been declining for years, not from shooting but due to continued loss of habitat, and now its long-term survival is uncertain.

Yellow Wattlebirds remain common in eucalypt forest and woodland across mainland Tasmania. With their tails fanned and long, pendulous wattles dancing about their face, these exquisite Tasmanian birds are a delight to see and hear – and nowadays, thankfully, too expensive to cook.

YELLOW-THROATED HONEYEATER

Lichenostomus flavicollis

The Yellow-throated Honeyeater is another of Tasmania's striking endemic birds. Its joyous call and rich colouring are distinctive and no matter where you journey on this island, you're likely to see and hear them.

Yellow-throated Honeyeaters are widespread in most types of forest, woodland and scrub; in fact just about anywhere there are large flowering plants. They seldom, if ever, form large flocks and are usually seen singly or in pairs. For most of the year they are sedentary and maintain permanent territories with a density of about one bird per hectare (Higgins *et al.* 2001). Their plumage is olive green above fading to grey below and the sexes are difficult to distinguish. Their Latin name *flavicollis* means 'yellow neck', but this inadequately describes the colour of their throat, which is a stunning rich, golden yellow called 'gamboge'. Their call is liquid and cheerful with eight distinct vocalisations and three types of song (Higgins *et al.* 2001), the commonest being a 'persistent flutter ending with chook', although that's not how it is formally described. Subtle dialects can be heard across the state which always catch you by surprise. For example, birds at Birchs Inlet, south of Macquarie Harbour, have an extra series of notes between the trill song and the tonk song, causing listeners to turn their head and say, 'What was that?'

The breeding season starts around September and it is typically the female who builds the large, cup-shaped nest from bark and grasses, cleverly disguised with spider webs and lined with soft bedding to cradle the eggs. The lining can be wallaby or possum fur, sheep's wool or even hair plucked from unwary people's heads. One photograph in Sharland (1971) shows a nest lavishly lined with bristles stolen from the back of a large white pig. The female lays two to three spotted chestnut red to purplish grey eggs, which she incubates alone, although she is closely attended by her partner. After the chicks are fledged, the romance is over and the adult male immediately evicts the entire family from his territory, and searches for a new mate to start a second clutch.

With their characteristic undulating flight, Yellow-throated Honeyeaters move through the foliage with ease, frequently stopping and hanging upside down to glean for spiders, beetles and other titbits among the branches, or hunting above the canopy with a twisting, turning motion. At certain times of the year they eat soft, over-ripe fruits, and 'In several districts in Northern Tasmania where small fruit growing is rather extensively gone in for, this Honey-eater is considered a perfect pest during the spring and summer months, owing to the ravages it makes among the cherries, currants, and gooseberries. Its local name in these districts is the Green Cherry-Picker.' (Littler 1910)

Tasmania's Yellow-throated Honeyeater shares a close evolutionary relationship with the White-eared Honeyeater *Lichenostomus leucotis* found more widely across eastern and southwestern Australia (Higgins *et al.* 2001). Both have similar plumage, behaviour and foraging habits, and it is clear that at one time they both shared a common ancestor when Tasmania and mainland Australia were joined. They also both have hair-pulling tendencies, although I don't think that's counted.

STRONG-BILLED & BLACK-HEADED HONEYEATERS

Melithreptus validirostris & Melithreptus affinis

Honeyeaters dominate our birdscape, with about seventy-three species found Australia wide. They vary in size and call, and all are attracted to a range of flowering plants. Active among the foliage, they use their sturdy bills and long, flexible tongues to extract nectar or probe for insects, each species exploiting a niche unique to it. The Strong-billed Honeyeater and Black-headed Honeyeater often feed together in Tasmania's tall eucalypt trees, although they never stay long and chatter constantly as they feed.

There are many similarities between the Strong-billed Honeyeater and Black-headed Honeyeater. Both endemic species were named by John Gould after his visit to Van Diemen's Land in 1838, and he, like others, recognised that they were attracted more to insects than flowers, gleaning them from under bark and the trunks of trees. The Strong-billed Honeyeater is particularly adept at this feeding behaviour and 'The agility with which it runs up and down the perpendicular stems of the trees, poking its bill into the crevices of the bark and detaching loose pieces, is wonderful. I have seen them so plentiful in a belt of thick scrub that the noise of their beaks and feet on the loose dry bark sounded like the pattering of dogs on dry leaves. While feeding a somewhat sharp whistling note is frequently uttered, in addition to which a fair amount of quarrelling is continually going on' (Littler 1910).

Both have solid, compact bodies, with the Strong-billed Honeyeater being slightly larger in size and weight (170 mm and 26 g compared to 145 mm and 18 g) (Higgins *et al.* 2001). Their plumage is dappled shades of olive green to grey brown dominated by a striking black cap that accentuates their eye. In the Strong-billed Honeyeater this cap is broken by a band of white extending across the back of the head and tapering above the eye in a stunning turquoise arch. This is further offset by a white chin rising in a delicate curve to the base of the bill.

Both species breed from August to December, with a clutch size of three to four eggs. Their deep, cup-shaped nests are usually woven by the female from bark and mosses and are well hidden amid the foliage at the end of a branch. They are often lined with the soft flowering heads of grasses or other bits and pieces such as sheep's wool or even cotton. 'As I sat on the veranda, I watched a black-headed honeyeater pulling and tugging at the worn threads of the Tibetan prayer flag I had strung across the railing … it was the blue flag I think … how marvellous these exquisite little creatures continue their lives by using what's around them' (Suzanne Skira pers. comm.). Incubation lasts about fifteen days and the chicks leave the nest a further fifteen days later. Their nests are often parasitised by cuckoos, which evict the honeyeaters' eggs to lay their own.

Outside of the breeding season, the two species become nomadic and form small, wandering flocks that burst into chatter as they move from tree to tree. While there is often overlap in the places they visit, the Strong-billed Honeyeater prefers the heavier forests at higher altitudes whereas the Black-headed Honeyeater is more abundant in the drier, open forests and woodlands of the east. Both species exploit parks and gardens and have coped well with European settlement.

DUSKY ROBIN

Melanodryas vittata

Old-timers knew these birds as the stump robin, because if there was gardening to be done, they would perch on a stump nearby and pounce as soon as the soil was turned. Even now the term 'robin' is used nostalgically to describe all the brightly coloured birds in the Petroica family, as they are just like the robin redbreasts of Britain. The Australian robins, however, are more closely aligned to the old world flycatchers, a large group of insectivorous birds found throughout Europe, Africa, Asia and Australasia (Higgins & Peter 2002).

Jean René Quoy and Joseph Gaimard described the Dusky Robin in 1830, after returning from their voyage to Van Diemen's Land aboard the *Astrolabe*. During their stay, they travelled extensively throughout the colony collecting many plant and animal specimens, and while this small bird may have seemed a little disappointing in appearance, it was uniquely Tasmanian and found in no other museum collection.

Dusky Robins live in most forest types at all altitudes, but generally prefer open woodland. They use forest margins and tracks, and have adapted to farmland and the urban fringe. While at first they appear ordinary, the adult's plumage is subtle shades of brown blending to a diffuse cream with a white bar on the wing, which provides excellent camouflage in forest. The juveniles are also well disguised but are markedly different, having heavy, pale streaks over most of their body. The male and female robins are similar in size and colour and almost impossible to differentiate. On average they are 155 mm in height and 27 g in weight. This makes them up to 15 mm taller and 15 g heavier than all other Tasmanian robins (Higgins & Peter 2002), and gives them their characteristic 'stand-tall' posture and stout appearance.

The Dusky Robin is a sedentary bird or, as Fletcher called them, the stay-at-home robin (Fletcher 1956), as they do not migrate. Their social organisation is poorly known due to the difficulty in distinguishing between the sexes, but at various times they can be seen singly, in pairs or in small flocks, and it is thought that the pairs stay together year after year. Banding studies have shown that they can live for at least five years, but it's more likely that they live up to nine or ten years, like other robin species. In character, they are curious and trusting, but will feign injury or mob any intruder that ventures too near their nest (Higgins & Peter 2002). That's when the extra 15 g comes in handy.

Nests are usually made in an old tree stump and are a rather untidy cup shape, fashioned to fit the hole. They are woven from strips of bark and fern frond, bound with spider webs, and lined with rootlets, fur, feathers or bits and pieces such as old string. The birds normally lay three to four eggs, which are incubated for about fifteen days. After raising their young, the Dusky Robins resume their position on the fence post, from where their continuous plaintive call hangs on the air with a melancholy tone.

2K
2Y
2B
100% Y

9564
56R

100% B

BLACK CURRAWONG

Strepera fuliginosa

Tasmania's Black Currawong has a sleek body, powerful bill and electric yellow eyes. Behind those eyes are extremely intelligent birds that have learned to use tools and manipulate humans.

Affectionately called the black jay or mountain jay, the Black Currawong is a mountain-loving species and is typically associated with rugged country and wild places. Its song 'carries across the mountains and valleys with a windswept sound … so exhilarating … shouted from crag to crag, in the sun drenched forests of the slopes … and on the moors carpeted with snow' (Sharland 1971). Its movements are seasonal and as winter approaches many come down from the high country to congregate in the woodlands or on the edge of towns. Noisy flocks of eighty or more birds regularly descend upon paddocks and can persist there for days, turning sods, chasing insects and chattering all the while.

Few studies have been conducted on the Black Currawong, which is surprising given that it is widespread, abundant and curious in nature. Two subspecies are known to exist. *Strepera fuliginosa parvior* is found to the east on Flinders Island and *S.f. colei* to the west on King Island, this population being by far the most restricted and now under threat of extinction. Despite being poorly known, the Black Currawong's habits are likely to be similar to those of the closely related Grey Currawong *Strepera versicolor* and Pied Currawong *Strepera graculina*, both of which occur on mainland Australia.

All the species form pairs that stay together year after year (Higgins *et al.* 2006). Black Currawongs breed from September to October and each season they build a large, bowl-shaped stick nest high in the fork of a tree. The female lays a small clutch of two to four purple to pale brown eggs, which hatch after about twenty days. The growing chicks have an insatiable appetite and produce a relentless, monotonous drone as they beg for food. After weeks of tireless labour, the weary parents begin to drop food in front of the chicks, rather than feeding them directly, in a clever ploy to encourage them out of the nest and to fend for themselves. Banding studies have shown that Black Currawongs can live for at least twelve years and it is more than likely that they live for twenty years or more, like the other currawong species (Higgins *et al.* 2006).

During the winter months, Black Currawongs feed mainly on fruits, seeds and insects but in spring they add a little flesh to their diet, hunting small nestlings, reptiles and rodents with cunning and stealth. Their powerful hooked beak is a precision tool and anything they can't swallow whole they will wedge on a stick and rip to pieces (Higgins *et al.* 2006). Whatever they can't digest is discarded in a regurgitated pellet that is crammed full of the skins of fruits or the bones of their victims.

Currawongs have a reputation for moving in and taking over and are audacious and cheeky, characteristics typical of the group. The suburbs are a smorgasbord of food and whatever the birds want, they take. One report has them stealing small articles from a campsite, including cutlery and pieces of soap, and they have even been observed taking workers' lunches (Higgins *et al.* 2006). Householders who regularly leave food out often note just how quickly the currawongs repel the smaller birds and that they are always the first to swoop. But as more and more food is left for them, it's easy to see who is training whom!

PEDRA BRANCA SKINK

Niveoscincus palfreymani

Pedra Branca is a remote, rocky islet 26 km off the southern tip of Tasmania. Windswept and rugged, the island is home to a unique species of lizard, stranded for thousands of years since the last ice age. Through its enforced isolation, this skink has evolved a fascinating way of life intrinsically linked to the seabirds that surround it.

Access to Pedra Branca is difficult, as the seas are rough and the weather changeable. Barely 52 m high and 2.5 ha in size, the island is formed by ledges and overhangs and is virtually devoid of any soil or vegetation. Its flattened top is used by Australasian Gannet *Sula serrator* and Shy Albatross *Thalassarche cauta* as a nesting site and for thousands of years their droppings have washed over the sandstone surface, giving rise to its Portuguese name meaning 'white rock'.

The Pedra Branca Skink belongs to an ancestral group of lizards that radiated to the cool-temperature regions of the South Pacific during the Quaternary period (Hutchinson *et al.* 2001). As the sea level rose, the skink became marooned on this tiny island, making it one of the rarest and most restricted animals in the world today. They are a powerfully built creature and grow to about 10 cm in body length. Their limbs are sturdy but their toes are long and slender, ideally suited to clinging in stormy weather. Incubation of eggs is impossible in this hostile environment and so they give birth to well-developed live young. They mature by about six years of age and can live for maybe ten to fifteen years (Threatened Species Unit 2001).

There are six main colonies of Pedra Branca Skink, clustered around burrows and crevices formed in the catacombed rock. Because the island can be washed by gigantic waves, these burrows are critical for survival and the skinks fight vigorously to acquire and defend them. On sunny days or whenever the temperature rises, Pedra Branca Skinks emerge from their burrows to bask. They constantly shuffle their position to maximise exposure to the sun's rays and sometimes they congregate on communal rocks where their bodies intertwine in a mass of moving parts. As soon as the temperature falls they quickly retreat to their burrows to hibernate or await the next glimpses of sun.

For most of the year, Pedra Branca Skinks feed on kelp flies caught in the lower reaches of the spray zone. But as the seabirds return to breed, the island springs to life, and the skinks now move to where the seabirds feed their young. In bursts of frenetic activity they scavenge scraps of fish as they spill from the chicks' mouths and onto the nests below, gorging themselves like miniature dinosaurs. This rich source of food and their specialised feeding behaviour have enabled the skink to survive in an environment which otherwise has little else to sustain them.

For thousands of years, the skinks and seabirds on Pedra Branca have lived in harmony, their populations fluctuating in natural cycles. Although the island is protected by World Heritage Area status, sadly the oceans are not, and in modern times new threats have emerged. More and more seabirds are being killed by marine pollution, entanglement and drowning on longline hooks; the natural balance is changing. In 2006, the population of Pedra Branca Skinks numbered fewer than 500 individuals and the species was listed nationally as vulnerable to extinction. A recovery plan has been prepared, but there is no money for its implementation.

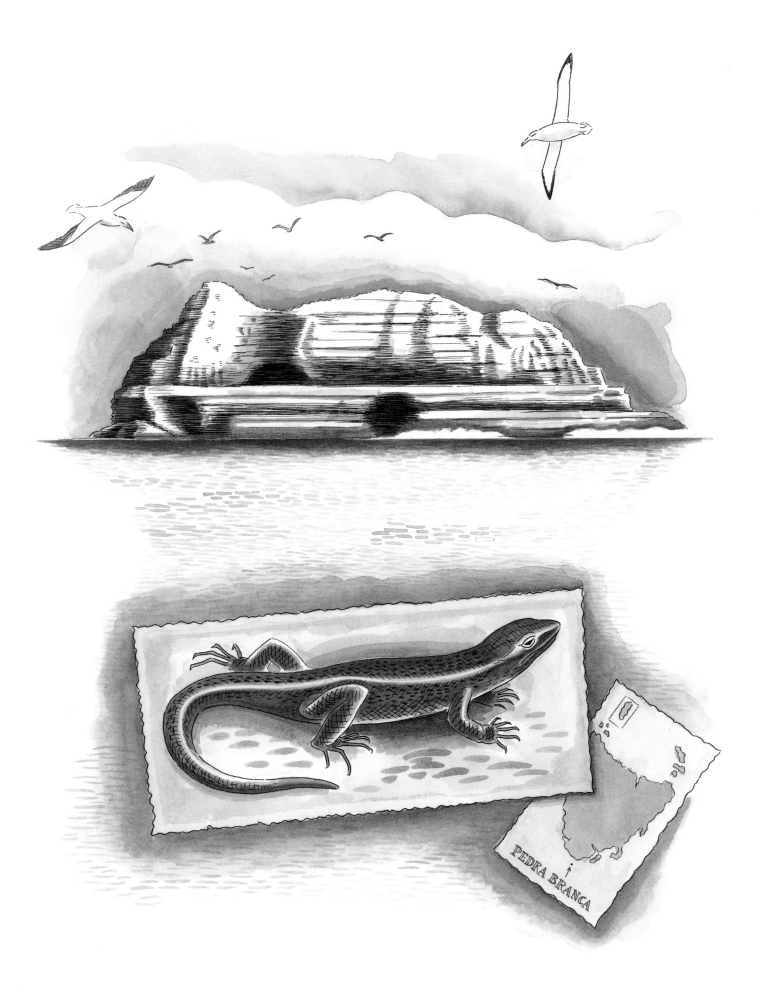

TASMANIAN TREE FROG

Litoria burrowsae

While strolling around Dove Lake, Miss Myrtle Burrows happened to notice two little frogs clinging to a buttongrass stem. It was 7 January 1941 and she had been spending the new year holidaying at Cradle Mountain. She collected the frogs and returned a week later to collect a third, a larger male from Wombat Tarn near Crater Lake. Miss Myrtle's curiosity and keen eye led to the discovery of a new species of frog for the state, the first in seventy-five years, and in her honour the Tasmanian Tree Frog *Litoria burrowsae* is named.

Dr Eric O. G. Scott, Director of the Queen Victoria Museum, formally described the species as elegant and handsome, with an immaculate thigh and groin and seven to nine close-set but rather blunt, slightly recurved teeth (Scott 1942). Its flanks and underside were granular and yellowish grey-brown in colour, with a dark stripe through the nostril and the eye. As more specimens were collected, the body colour was found to vary between a uniform bright green and a camouflaged, mottled pattern resembling that of lichen.

The Tasmanian Tree Frog belongs to the family Hylidae and is a true climbing species. Its fingers and toes are partly webbed and each tiny digit ends in a large terminal disc or suction pad, enabling it to climb vertical surfaces as smooth as glass. Though most individuals live on the ground near water, some have been discovered as high as 30 m in the tops of tall eucalypts.

Tasmanian Tree Frogs breed in spring and summer or occasionally after heavy rains. The female can lay up to 120 eggs clustered around vegetation like tiny bunches of grapes and when the tadpoles emerge about six days later, they have elaborate mouthparts for grazing on algae and other plant material. It takes up to eight months for the tadpoles to grow into froglets and a further three to six months for them to reach adult body size (about 60 mm) and develop their attractive green colour and faint curry odour (Littlejohn 2003). As with most amphibians, only the males call, and they make a loud goose-like *quank quank quank*.

Though their species names have changed, Scott speculated in 1942 that the Tasmanian Tree Frog was the high-altitude counterpart of the Green and Gold Bell Frog *Litoria raniformis*, found more commonly throughout the northeast, Midlands and coastal lowlands. He was correct, as *L. burrowsae* occurs mainly throughout the western half of Tasmania in high-altitude rainforest, wet forest, alpine meadows and sedge.

Frogs are well-known indicators of environmental health, but sadly too few people have listened to their call, as now frogs and toads all over the world are declining at an alarming rate. Chytrid Fungus *Batrachochytrium dendrobatidis* is a lethal frog disease that destroys their mouthparts and skin and has already caused the extinction of one Australian frog species and been implicated in the decline of several others. Chytrid Fungus was first detected in Tasmania in 2004 and since then has been confirmed in nearly all of Tasmania's eleven native frogs, including the Tasmanian Tree Frog. Two species of Tasmanian frog are threatened with extinction, though sadly more will probably follow.

PEDDER GALAXIAS

Galaxias pedderensis

Over a twenty-year period, an ecological disaster unfolded which very nearly resulted in the extinction of another of Tasmania's unique native species, the Pedder Galaxias. This seldom-told story embodies one of the great ironies in conservation history, for it involves the salvation of a species, yet the tragic loss of a wild and beautiful place.

The story begins in the late 1960s when the State Government and Hydro Electric Commission joined forces to build a new power scheme. In 1967, when the majestic Lake Pedder, the jewel in the southwest crown, had its status as a National Park revoked, conservationists became suspicious and concerned. By the early 1970s a public campaign was under way, condemning the proposal as environmental vandalism. The government reassured the public that the development was in their best interest, as it would attract investment to the state and cause minimal environmental damage. Lake Pedder became a symbol and a battleground and angry protests raged both on water and the streets of Hobart. The campaign spread nationally, then internationally, as images of the lake's natural beauty caused people to cry in disbelief that such an action was being contemplated, let alone might actually happen. But it was and it did. In 1972, construction on a dam commenced and Lake Pedder was flooded to provide an extra 60 megawatts of electricity. The lake and its natural ecosystem would change forever.

Just as scientists predicted, in the first few years after flooding there was an initial explosion in Pedder Galaxias numbers, as it was a case of more food equals more fish. However, surveys conducted during the early 1980s reported that the species was becoming increasingly difficult to find. The damming of Lake Pedder and the upper Serpentine River had not only destroyed the species' natural lowland spawning habitat but it also enabled two predatory fish to establish. Brown Trout *Salmo trutta* and the Climbing Galaxias *Galaxias brevipinnis* not only increased competition for the Pedder Galaxias but also ate its eggs and larvae. By 1989 the Pedder Galaxias had completely disappeared from the newly created waterway and could only be found in four of its original tributaries. One year later, the species was confined to two small feeder streams and was on the brink of extinction.

Early efforts to save the species were hampered by a lack of knowledge. An artificial breeding tank, dubbed the 'passion pond', was unable to hatch eggs collected from the wild or replicate the species' migratory stage (Hamr 1992). It was thought that the lake environment acted as a nursery for pelagic larvae and juveniles and when the temperature rose in spring, adults would migrate upstream to spawn in the tributaries.

By 1991, a desperate act was needed. With little time to undertake baseline surveys, scientists released thirty-four adult fish into Lake Oberon in Tasmania's Western Arthurs Range. It was just as well, because by 1996 no fish could be found in either the Lake Pedder impoundment or any of its former tributaries. Tasmania's endemic Pedder Galaxias was now 'extinct in the wild'.

Years later the Lake Oberon population is thriving and at last count had increased to about 500 individuals (Threatened Species Section 2006c). While a small surplus of fish has enabled further relocations to be attempted, to date these have been slow to establish and the relocated fish are yet to breed. So, just like the campaign to restore Lake Pedder to its former glory, this conservation battle will rage for a long time yet.

References

Apthorp, S. (1992), 'Maria Island's restless natives', *Leatherwood* No 4: 46–51.

Baird, R. F. (1984), 'The Pleistocene distribution of the Tasmanian Native-hen *Gallinula mortierii mortierii*', *Emu* 84: 119–123.

Brasil, L. (1914), 'The emu of King Island', *Emu* 14: 88–97.

Brereton, R., Mallick, S. A. and Kennedy, S. J. (2004), 'Foraging preferences of Swift Parrots on Tasmanian Blue-gum: tree size, flowering frequency and flowering intensity', *Emu* 104: 377–383.

Brown, P. B. and Wilson, R. I. (1980), 'A survey of the Orange-bellied Parrot (*Neophema chrysogaster*) in Tasmania, Victoria and South Australia', National Parks & Wildlife Service, Tasmania.

Brown, P. B. and Wilson, R. I. (1982), 'The Orange-bellied Parrot', in Groves, R. H. and Ride, W. D. L. (Eds), *Species at risk*, Australian Academy of Science, Canberra.

Bryant, S. L. (1988), 'Maintenance and captive breeding of the Eastern Quoll, *Dasyurus viverrinus*', *International Zoo Yearbook* 27: 119–124.

Bryant, S. L. and Jackson, J. (1999), *Tasmania's threatened fauna handbook: What, where and how to conserve Tasmania's threatened animals*, Threatened Species Unit, Department of Primary Industries, Water and Environment, Tasmania.

Cronin, L. (1991), *Key guide to Australian mammals*, Reed Books, NSW.

Cumpston, J. S. (1968), *Macquarie Island*, ANARE Scientific Reports, Series A(1), Antarctic Division, Australia.

DCE (1992), *Extinct Mammals 2*, Action Statement No 14, Department of Conservation and Environment, Victoria.

Dickman, C. and Woodford Ganf, R. (2007), *A fragile balance: the extraordinary story of Australian marsupials*, Craftsman House, NSW.

Donaghey, R. H. (Ed), (2003), *The fauna of King Island: A guide to identification and conservation management*, King Island Natural Resource Management Group, King Island.

Dove, H. S. (1926), 'How Tasmania lost the emu', *Emu* 25: 213.

Driessen, M. M. and Rose, R. K. (1999) '*Pseudomys higginsi*', *Mammalian Species* 623: 1–5.

Fletcher, J. A. (1956), *Tasmania's own birds*, Mercury Press Pty Ltd, Hobart.

Fuller, E. (2000), *Extinct birds*, Oxford University Press, Oxford.

Gould, J. F. R. S. (1848), *The Birds of Australia*, 7 vols, 36 parts, 600 plates, London, 1840–1848.

Green, R. H. (1960), 'Extinct *Dromaius* species', *Emu* 60: 19.

Green, R. H. (1968), 'The murids and small dasyurids in Tasmania, Part 3', *Records of the Queen Victoria Museum* No 32: 1–11.

Green, R. H. (1995), *The fauna of Tasmania: Birds*, Potoroo Publishing, Launceston.

Guiler, E. R. (1985), *Thylacine: The tragedy of the Tasmanian tiger*, Oxford University Press, Melbourne.

Guiler, E. R. (1986), 'The Beaumaris zoo in Hobart', *Papers & Proceedings Tasmanian Historical Research Association* 33(4): 121–176.

Hamr, P. (1992), 'The Pedder Galaxias', *Australian Natural History* 23(12): 904.

Harris, S., Buchanan, A. and Connolly, A. (2001), *One hundred islands: the flora of the outer Furneaux*, Department of Primary Industries, Water and Environment, Tasmania.

Higgins, E. T. & Petterd, W. F. (1883), 'Descriptions of hitherto undescribed Antechini and Muridae inhabiting Tasmania', *Papers & Proceedings of the Royal Society of Tasmania* 1882: 171–176.

Higgins, P. J. (Ed) (1999), *Handbook of Australian, New Zealand and Antarctic birds, Volume 4 Parrots to dollarbird*, Oxford University Press, Melbourne.

Higgins, P. J. and Peter, J. M. (Eds) (2002), *Handbook of Australian, New Zealand and Antarctic Birds, Volume 6 Pardalotes to shrike-thrushes*, Oxford University Press, Melbourne.

Higgins, P. J., Peter, J. M. and Cowling, S. J. (Eds) (2006), *Handbook of Australian, New Zealand and Antarctic Birds, Volume 7 Boatbill to starlings*, Oxford University Press, Melbourne.

Higgins, P. J., Peter, J. M. & Steele, W. K. (Eds) (2001), *Handbook of Australian, New Zealand and Antarctic Birds, Volume 5 Tyrant-flycatchers to chats*, Oxford University Press, Melbourne.

Hindwood, K. A. (1938), 'John Gould in Australia', *Emu* 38(2): 95–117.

Hope, J. H. (1974), 'The biogeography of the mammals of the islands of Bass Strait', in W. D. Williams (Ed), *Biogeography and ecology of Tasmania*, Chapter 14, Dr W. Junk, The Hague.

Hutchinson, M., Swain, R. and Driessen, M. (2001), *Snakes and lizards of Tasmania, Fauna of Tasmania Handbook No 9*, University of Tasmania, Hobart.

Jones, M. E., Rose, R. K. and Burnett, S. (2001), '*Dasyurus maculatus*', *Mammalian Species* 676: 1–9.

Jouventin, P. and Lequette, B. (1990), 'The dance of the Wandering Albatross *Diomedea exulans*', *Emu* 90(2): 123–131.

Legge, W. V. (1907), 'The emus of Tasmania and King Island', *Emu* 6: 116–119.

Littlejohn, M. J. (2003), *Frogs of Tasmania. Fauna of Tasmania Handbook No 6*, University of Tasmania, Hobart.

Littler, F. M. (1910), *A Handbook of the birds of Tasmania and its dependencies*, published by the author, Launceston, Tasmania.

Lord, C. E. & Scott, H. H. (1924), *A synopsis of the vertebrate animals of Tasmania*, Oldham, Beddome & Meredith, Hobart.

Macdonald, J. D. (1962), 'Specimens of extinct Tasmanian Emu', *Emu* 61(4): 333.

Marchant, S. & Higgins, P. J. (Eds) (1990), *Handbook of Australian, New Zealand and Antarctic Birds, Volume 1 Ratites to ducks*, Oxford University Press, Melbourne.

Marchant, S. & Higgins, P. J. (Eds) (1993), *Handbook of Australian, New Zealand and Antarctic Birds, Volume 2 Raptors to lapwings*, Oxford University Press, Melbourne.

Mawson, D. (1934), *The home of the blizzard*, Hodder & Stoughton Ltd, London.

Midlands Bushweb (2003), *The nature of the Midlands*, Artemis Publishing, Hobart.

Mooney, N. (1997), 'Habitat and seasonality of nesting Masked Owls in Tasmania', pp 34–39 in G. Czechura and S. Debus (Eds), *Australian Raptor Studies 2, Birds Australia Monograph 3*, Birds Australia, Melbourne.

Olsen, P. D. (1995), *Australian birds of prey*, UNSW Press, Sydney.

Owen, D. (2003), *Thylacine: the tragic tale of the Tasmanian tiger*, Allen & Unwin, NSW.

Rose, R. W. (1987), 'Reproductive biology of the Tasmanian Bettong (*Bettongia gaimardi*: Macropodidae)', *Journal of Zoology* (London) 212: 59–67.

Scott, E. O. G. (1942), 'A new Hyla from Cradle Valley Tasmania', *Records of the Queen Victoria Museum*, Launceston 1(1): 5–11.

SDAC (1996), *State of the Environment Tasmania, Vol 1 – conditions and trends*, Sustainable Development Advisory Council, Department of Environment and Land Management, Tasmania.

Sharland, M. (1963), *Tasmanian Wildlife*, Melbourne University Press, Victoria.

Sharland, M. (1971), *A pocketful of nature*, Mercury-Walch Pty Ltd, Hobart, Tasmania.

SPRT (2008), *Swifts across the Strait Newsletter*, Swift Parrot Recovery Team, NSW.

Taylor, R. H. (1979), 'How the Macquarie Island Parakeet became extinct', *New Zealand Journal of Ecology* 2: 42–45.

Terauds, A., Gales, R., Baker, B. and Alderman, R. (2006), 'Population and survival trends of Wandering Albatrosses (*Diomedea exulans*) breeding on Macquarie Island', *Emu* 106: 211–218.

Terauds, A. and Stewart, F. (2008), *Subantarctic wilderness: Macquarie Island*, Allen & Unwin, NSW.

The Mercury (1974), 'Bones revive another story of extinction', The world of 'Peregrine', *Mercury Magazine*, undated.

The Mercury (2009), 'Minister thinks parrot doomed', the *Mercury* Newspaper, Hobart, 12 March, p 9.

Threatened Species Section (2006a), *Threatened Tasmanian Eagles Recovery Plan 2006–2010*, Department of Primary Industries and Water, Hobart.

Threatened Species Section (2006b), *Fauna Recovery Plan: Forty-Spotted Pardalote 2006–2010*, Department of Primary Industries and Water, Hobart.

Threatened Species Section (2006c), *Recovery Plan: Tasmanian Galaxiidae 2006–2010*, Department of Primary Industries & Water, Hobart.

Threatened Species Unit (2001), *Pedra Branca Skink Recovery Plan*, Department of Primary Industries, Water and Environment, Hobart.

Troughton, E. (1967), *Furred animals of Australia*, Ninth edition, Angus & Robertson, Sydney.

Van Tets, G. F. (1978), 'Pleistocene cave material of Tasmanian Native-hen *Tribonyx mortierii* and Sooty Shearwater *Puffinus griseus* in Tasmania', *Records of the Queen Victoria Museum* 59: 1–4.

Visoiu, M. and Lloyd, S. (2003), 'Bugs, birds, bettongs and bush: maintaining habitat for fauna in Tasmania', Kit 10 of the Tasmanian Bushcare Toolkit, Nature Conservation Report 03/4, Department of Primary Industries, Water and Environment, Tasmania.

West, J. (1852), *The history of Tasmania*, Royal Australian Historical Society, Sydney, Angus & Robertson, 1971 edition.

Acknowledgments

Sincere thanks to Janine Flew and Ian Woodward for editing and proofreading the text and continually reminding me about grammatical stuff, which I still haven't grasped. Thank you to my dear friends and colleagues, especially Peter Marmion, Chris Tzaros, Mark Holdsworth, Nick Mooney, Stephen Harris, Suzanne Skira, Sophie Marshall Pru Cotton and Margie and Steve Bryant, who continually encouraged me along the way. Thank you to the talented graphic designer Tracey Allen and to the Quintus Board for making this book happen. To the wonderful Tim Squires for his bond of friendship and the vision we shared. Most of all I thank Janine Long and Paul Wilson, two inspiring people who guided me back to where the birds sing.

Sally Bryant

This has been a long journey and there are many people to thank. Kathryn Medlock of the Tasmanian Museum and Art Gallery, and Catherine Kemper of the South Australian Muscum, provided access to the zoological treasures in their care. Wildlife photographer Dave Watts provided some valuable reference material. David Owen, Ralph Crane, Andrew Hopwood and everyone at Quintus Publishing have turned this dream into a reality. Graphic designer Tracey Allen has excelled in all aspects of the design and production. Artist Ron Brooks has provided invaluable advice and encouragement. Sally Bryant has written beautifully, and been a great friend and team mate along the way. My family and friends have all been terrific support – thank you all. And special thanks to my very patient wife, Teresa, and our treasured little wild things, Eva and Ruby.

Tim Squires